Memoirs of a Man's Maiden Years

Memoirs of a Man's Maiden Years

N. O. BODY

Translated by Deborah Simon
Preface by Sander L. Gilman
Afterword by Hermann Simon

PENN

University of Pennsylvania Press
Philadelphia

Originally published 1907 as *Aus eines Mannes Mädchenjahren* by Gustav Rieckes Buchhandlung, Nachfolger

English translation, preface, and afterword copyright © 2006 University of Pennsylvania Press
Printed in the United States of America on acid-free paper

10 9 8 7 6 5 4 3 2 1

Published by
University of Pennsylvania Press
Philadelphia, Pennsylvania 19104-4112

Library of Congress Cataloging-in-Publication Data

Body, N. O., 1885–1956.
   [Aus eines Mannes Mädchenjahren. English]
   Memoirs of a man's maiden years / N. O. Body ; preface by Sander L. Gilman ; afterword by Hermann Simon ; translated by Deborah Simon.
      p. cm.
   Includes bibliographical references.
   ISBN-10: 0-8122-3908-3 (cloth : alk. paper)
   ISBN-13: 978-0-8122-3908-9
   1. Body, N. O., 1885–1956. 2. Sexual orientation. 3. Sex (Psychology)
4. Hermaphroditism. I. Title.
HQ23.B8213 2006
306.76´0943—dc22

                                                                    2005042333

Contents

Preface
Whose Body Is It, Anyway?
Hermaphrodites, Gays, and Jews
in N. O. Body's Germany

SANDER L. GILMAN

"N. O. Body" is a most appropriate pseudonym for Karl M. Baer (1885–1956) to have used when he sat down to pen his autobiography, which appeared in 1907.[1] For being "nobody" was his way of seeing his body. It was doubly alienated ("nobody" is English rather than German) as it was male as well as female, Jewish as well as German. This is how he imagined his past life raised as a woman, Martha Baer, in a Jewish family in Imperial Germany. But it is "nobody" that Odysseus tricks the Cyclops into answering when asked who has harmed him: "Who has hurt you?" "Nobody," the blinded giant responds. In his autobiography, Baer is simultaneously the clever trickster but also the damaged giant.

1. On Baer specifically, see David Brenner, "Re(-)dressing the 'German-Jewish': A Jewish Hermaphrodite in Wilhelmine Germany," in *Borders, Exiles, and Diasporas*, ed. Elazar Barkan and Marie-Denise Shelton (Stanford, Calif.: Stanford University Press, 1998), pp. 32–45. On hermaphrodism in culture, see Stefan Hirschauer, *Die soziale Konstruktion der Transsexualität: Über die Medizin und den Geschlechtswechsel* (Frankfurt am Main: Suhrkamp, 1993); Gesa Lindemann, *Das paradoxe Geschlecht: Transsexualität im Spannungsfeld von Körper, Leib und Gefühl* (Frankfurt am Main: Fischer Taschenbuch Verlag, 1993); Annette Runte, *Biographische Operationen: Diskurse der Transsexualität* (Munich:

On its surface, Baer's autobiography is a remarkable fin-de-siècle document of "hermaphrodism," as the Berlin sexologist Magnus Hirschfeld (1868–1935) notes in his epilogue. Its subject suffered from false gender assignment because of the apparent ambiguity of his genitalia as an infant. He was registered and treated as a female child rather than a male child, an error of assignment that became evident only at puberty. He was a "pseudohermaphrodite," to use the terminology of the day, as his body was hormonally and psychologically gendered male, even though his genitalia seemed at first glance ambiguous. Sex was defined by the appearance of the body and was dimorphic: there were men, and there were women. Anyone who was neither or both was seen as pathological.

The central argument of the autobiography is expressed on its opening page: "One may raise a healthy boy in as womanish a manner as one wishes, and a female creature in as mannish; never will this cause their senses to remain forever reversed." No confusion about gender can exist except, as is the case here, through the fuzzy ineptitude of the physician who at Baer's birth in 1885 (not 1884, as in the text) stated that "on superficial inspection, the shape has a feminine appearance; ergo we have a girl before us." But the autobiography shows that this was never the case. Baer was always a male, even when

---

W. Fink, 1996); Jay Prosser, *Second Skins: The Body Narratives of Transsexuality* (New York: Columbia University Press, 1998); Kate More and Stephen Whittle, *Reclaiming Genders: Transsexual Grammars at the Fin de Siècle* (London: Cassell, 1999); Jason Cromwell, *Transmen and FTMs: Identities, Bodies, Genders, and Sexualities* (Urbana: University of Illinois Press, 1999). Of extreme importance is the work of Alice Domurat Dreger: "Doubtful Sex: The Fate of the Hermaphrodite in Victorian Fiction," *Victorian Studies* 38 (1995): 335–70; *Hermaphrodites and the Medical Invention of Sex* (Cambridge, Mass.: Harvard University Press, 1998); "A History of Intersexuality: From the Age of Gonads to the Age of Consent," *Journal of Clinical Ethics* 9 (1998): 345–55; ed., *Intersex in the Age of Ethics* (Hagerstown, Md.: University Publishing Group, 1999); "Jarring Bodies: Thoughts on the Display of Unusual Anatomies," *Perspectives in Biology and Medicine* 43 (2000): 161–72.

treated as a female. As Hirschfeld notes in his epilogue: "The sex of a person lies more in his mind than in his body." For Baer, there was no ambiguity in his sense of discomfort as a woman caused by the outward appearance of his genitalia. His desires were male, from the games he wished to play to the women with whom he fell in love. But he had been assigned the gender role of a woman, which made his masculine desire seem perverse to him. The argument of the autobiography is that male children, however raised or treated, remain masculine in their intrinsic identity. This was very much against the tendency of the time and again against the practice of the late twentieth century.[2] Today this sounds extraordinarily prescient.

After the 1960s, gender-reassignment surgery of children with "ambiguous genitalia" followed the view of scientists such as the Johns Hopkins psychologist John Money, who argued that it was culture, not nature, that defined gender.[3] It became usual to alter the external genitalia of babies with ambiguous sexuality to the female because of its greater surgical simplicity. These children were treated with hormones and raised as females. Over the past decade, a substantial literature argues that Baer and Hirschfeld were right and Money was wrong. Gender is imprinted in, as well as on, the body: anatomy is not destiny. The primary case used by Money as his proof of the successful raising of a boy as a girl was that of David Reimer (known in popular culture as the case of John and Joan). He was one of two identical twins, whose botched circumcision in 1967 led to the amputation of his penis at eight months and his being raised as a girl. Money announced this as proof that culture was the sole determinant of gender.

2. Thus the famed Philadelphia surgeon Samuel David Gross (1805–84), the subject of Thomas Eakins's *The Gross Clinic*, undertook a castration and reconstruction in the 1850s. See S. D. Gross, "Case of Hermaphrodism, Involving the Operation of Castration and Illustrating a New Principle of Juridical Medicine," *American Journal of the Medical Sciences* n.s. 24 (1852): 386–90.

3. As early as his dissertation "Hermaphroditism: An Inquiry into the Nature of a Human Paradox" (diss., Harvard University, 1952).

At age twenty-five, Reimer demanded to have his sexual identity as a man reconstituted. He had always felt himself to be male even in his culturally and hormonally reinforced role as a woman. By the early twenty-first century, he had become a media darling, appearing on *Oprah*. In May 2004, he committed suicide at the age of thirty-eight.[4] His death was read as proof of how wrong Money was.

Reimer's life rebutted, as the first major reassessment of the case noted, the primary assumptions that everyone is psychosexually neutral at birth and that all healthy psychosexual development is dependent upon the appearance of the genitals.[5] This view, espoused by Money, argued from a set of assumptions based on the existence of hermaphrodites. He assumed that they were ungendered at birth. But who are these undifferentiated hermaphrodites? Do they not have a gendered identity from the very beginning of their lives? Is their understanding of the meaning of gender not also shaped by the historical world in which they are born? Certainly, this was the case for the world of the five-year-old "Martha" (Karl) Baer, who, like Reimer, much preferred the games and toys of boys to those of girls, even though the world treated him as it would a little girl.

The publication of Baer's autobiography in Germany is part of a fixation in the late nineteenth and early twentieth century with this surprisingly malleable category of the hermaphrodite. The freakish body, the body whose physiology did not reflect societal norms, has always fascinated European culture. From Petronius's representation in his *Satyricon* of hermaphrodites in first-century Rome to Velazquez's dwarf center stage in the Spanish court portrait *Las Meninas* (1656) to the fantasies about sexual desire in Victor Hugo's *The Hunchback of*

4. Mireya Navarro, "When Gender Isn't a Given," *New York Times*, Sunday Style section, September 19, 2004, pp. 1, 6.

5. Milton Diamond and H. Keith Sigmundson, "Sex Reassignment at Birth: A Long-Term Review and Clinical Implications," *Archives of Pediatric & Adolescent Medicine* 151 (1997): 298–304. A popular study is available by John Colapinto, *As Nature Made Him: The Boy Who Was Raised as a Girl* (New York: Perennial, 2002).

Notre Dame (1831), Europeans have stressed physical difference as a manner of defining the ever-changing boundaries of the "normal" and "healthy" body. Central to all of these representations was the need to "see" the physical difference of the body. Difference had to be physical even if the fascination was with the unseeable (and, in these terms, unknowable) aspects of what makes human beings different. Thus, ruminating about sexual desire and practices, such as homosexuality, which was in the process of becoming the subject of the medical gaze in the nineteenth century, did not have the same empirical claim as observing physical difference, such as that of the hermaphrodite.

In the late nineteenth century, there was an explosion of autobiographical accounts of sexual difference that attempted to translate a fascination with behavioral or social aspects of sexual difference into physiological terms. One of the central metaphors for this difference was that of the hermaphrodite. Virtually all of these attempts were cast as part of a new "medical" (or "forensic") attempt to understand the psyche of "perversion." Homosexuals could be judged only by their acts; there seemed to be no way of "seeing" their difference in contrast to the healthy, normal body. How could one identify the homosexual? Could he (and, at this point, the pervert was always male) be as visible as the hermaphrodite? In a medical model, the homosexual was inherently different from the healthy heterosexual, but was this difference an intrinsic one or could anyone be or become homosexual?

In the 1860s, the German lawyer Karl Ulrichs provided an alternative model for a nonjudgmental account of uranism, or homosexuality.[6] He hoped that this would free the homosexual from the moral or medical taint that accompanied any representation of "perverse" sexual attraction or activity in the evolving medical model. He sought to defuse the legal status of the homosexual as sexual criminal while avoiding the medicalization of homosexuality as a perversion. One can add that liberals such as Richard Kraft-Ebbing, in his 1886

6. Hubert Kennedy, *Ulrichs: The Life and Works of Karl Heinrich Ulrichs* (Boston: Alyson, 1988).

Psychopathia Sexualis, also wished to free the homosexual from the charges of criminal sexual activity or moral depravity by medicalizing it and thus providing therapy rather than prison as the alternative. Ulrichs's argument was that the homosexual (and his references are exclusively to male same-sex desire and activity) was a "third sex," a natural alternative to the two sexes, male and female.

By the end of the century, physicians such as Magnus Hirschfeld applied the model of the third sex and sought a biological rather than a theoretical model. Of special interest to Hirschfeld were the "intermediate" cases of sexuality, the model for which was the hermaphrodite, who, according to these accounts, was both female and male and thus neither male nor female.

Hirschfeld and the sexologists of the 1890s found it necessary to turn to the broader medical audience as well as the broader public with case material to prove their argument. While Michel Foucault had to excavate his famous mid-nineteenth-century case of the nineteenth-century French hermaphrodite Herculine Barbin from the Parisian archives of the Department of Public Health, it is much less difficult to find analogous cases of sexual difference in Germany after the 1890s.[7] This literature explodes in the medical literature of the day and quickly seeps into general public discourse.[8] The autobiographical literature on homosexuality, cast in the model of the third sex, uses the hermaphrodite as its concrete analogy for German consumption. The pioneer (and long-lived) sexologist Havelock Ellis published the first volume of his studies on sexuality collaboratively with the writer John Addington Symonds (1840–93) in Germany in 1896.[9]

7. Michel Foucault, ed., *Herculine Barbin: Being the Recently Discovered Memoirs of a Nineteenth-Century French Hermaphrodite*, trans. R. McDougall (New York: Pantheon, 1978).

8. See Klaus Müller, *Aber in meinem Herzen sprach eine Stimme so laut: Homosexuelle Autobiographien und medizinischen Pathographien im neunzehnten Jahrhundert* (Berlin: Rosa Winkel, 1991).

9. Havelock Ellis and J. A. Symonds, *Das konträre Geschlechtsgefühl* (Leipzig: G. Wigand, 1896).

Symonds's autobiographical account of "this question of Greek love in modern life" was the core of this work, which was published the next year in Great Britain, to the horror of his friends. Among the texts that Ellis included is a detailed summary of Ulrichs's views on homosexuality as an appendix to the German original (and anonymously in subsequent English editions).

By 1900, there were hundreds of autobiographical accounts of sexual anomalies, including hermaphrodism, available in technical literature and some in more popular literature. Magnus Hirschfeld's volume *Berlin's Third Sex*, with massive citations from autobiographies, appeared as volume three in the original urban sociological series Metropolitan Documents, widely sold in German bookstores prior to World War I.[10] This series, edited by Hans Ostwald, was the basis for many urban sociological studies of the 1910s and after. Most of these studies, like Hirschfeld's and Ellis's, cut and pasted these into "scientific" discourses about sexual difference as firsthand "proofs" of the nature of sexual difference. Here the hermaphrodite always served as the model for sexual difference. The "third sex" was like the hermaphrodite, in that it was to be found in nature.

This notion that the hermaphrodite can serve as the model for an understanding of male homosexuality is not merely an idiosyncrasy of the turn of the century. Michel Foucault writes in his *History of Sexuality* that "homosexuality appeared as one of the forms of sexuality when it was transposed from the practice of sodomy into a kind of interior androgyny, a hermaphrodism of the soul. The sodomite had been a temporary aberration; the homosexual was now a species."[11] This takes place in the 1890s, the world in which Karl Baer lived.

As a literary trope, the modern notion of hermaphrodism as metaphor for the impermanence of sexual dimorphism takes place at the same time. In 1891, we find a "magic seed" in Archibald Ganter and

10. Magnus Hirschfeld, *Berlins drittes Geschlecht* (Berlin: Hermann Seemann, n.d. [1905]).
11. Michel Foucault, *The History of Sexuality*, trans. Robert Hurley (New York: Vintage, 1980), 1:43.

Fergus Redmond's novel (and then a successful play) *A Florida En-chantment* that transforms the protagonist and her servant into men. But Victorian and early twentieth-century erotica often turned on the confusion of sexual roles, whether in the form of androgynous char-acters or transvestism. Thus in *"Frank" and I*, the reader discovers that the female lover of a young man turns out to be male; and in *Miss High-Heels*, the hero, Dennis Evelyn Beryl, is transformed by his sister into a woman. Such purposeful sexual confusion is also at the core of Agatha Christie's early novel *The Man in the Brown Suit* (1924). It is, of course, only in 1928 with Virginia Woolf's *Orlando* that the full promise of the metaphor of hermaphrodism for the instability of sexual iden-tity is played out.[12] After that, it becomes a commonplace in the liter-ature of the twentieth century.

In Germany, as in the rest of Europe, there was a steady stream of medical studies on hermaphrodism throughout the nineteenth century. But it is with Magnus Hirschfeld's work in the 1890s that the model character of homosexuality was stressed in such studies.[13] By then, the hermaphrodite had become not only a model for, but also the etiol-ogy of, homosexuality. At the beginning of the twentieth century, Hirschfeld published a long series of essays by Franz von Neugebauer (1856–1914) in his *Yearbook of Sexual Intermediate Stages*.[14]

Neugebauer was the most important commentator on the biologi-cal nature of hermaphrodism within Hirschfeld's model during this period. He argued that all children were born "bisexual" and that

12. See Barbara Wedekind-Schwertner, *"Daß ich eins und doppelt bin": Studien zur Idee der Androgynie unter besonderer Berücksichtigung Thomas Manns* (New York: Lang, 1984); Andrea Raehs, *Zur Ikonographie des Hermaphroditen: Begriff und Problem von Hermaphroditismus und Androgynie in der Kunst* (New York: Lang, 1990).

13. The best summary of his views is in his textbook: Magnus Hirschfeld, *Sexualpathologie: Ein Lehrbuch für Ärzte und Studierende* (Bonn: Marcus und Weber, 1917).

14. Neugebauer's work is wide-ranging; see his early work: F. L. Neugebauer, *Zur Lehre von den angeborenen und erworbenen Verwachsungen und Verengerungen*

homosexuality was an inherent quality of brain development. But he was also convinced that women who appeared to be male were less likely to have truly bisexual characteristics than a man who desired to appear as a woman. (The rationale is clear: Why would a high-status individual such as a male desire to be a low-status individual such as a woman? There is a social advantage to the latter but never to the former.) A gynecologist in Warsaw and chief of staff at the Evangelical Hospital there, Neugebauer had systematically collected "930 observations of hermaphrodism in human beings; 38 of these were cases which had come under my own observation, and the rest I found dispersed in ancient and modern literature."[15] In his work, he rethought the nosology of hermaphrodism. However, following Hirschfeld's model, he also understood the social consequences of such biological categorization. He clearly links hermaphrodism and homosexuality, as does Baer's image of the childhood sexual exploration and his young adult sense that he might be a lesbian: "It occurred to me alone, that I perhaps felt in that way." As Neugebauer argued, this is not an unusual sense of sexual confusion:

The male or female character of the genetic sense of pseudohermaphrodites depends very often on the sort of environment in which they are brought up, that is to say, upon whether they are educated as boys or girls; it must be set down entirely to the influence of suggestion if a male hermaphrodite, owing to mistaken sex brought up as a girl, afterwards shows a feminine genetic

---

der Scheide: Sowie des angeborenen Scheidenmangels mit Ausschluss der Doppelbildungen (Berlin: A. T. Engelhardt, 1895), through to his classic essay "58 Beobachtungen von periodischen genitalen Blutungen mestruellen Anschein, pseudomenstruellen Blutungen, Menstruatio vicaia, Molimina menstrualia usw. bei Scheinzwitter," *Jahrbuch für sexuallen Zwischenstufen* 6 (1904): 277–326. His views are summarized in his *Hermaphroditismus beim Menschen* (Leipzig: Werner Klinkhardt, 1908).

15. I cite from his English-language summary essay: Franz von Neugebauer, "Hermaphrodism in the Daily Practice of Medicine: Being Information upon Hermaphrodism Indispensable to the Practitioner," *British Gynaecological Journal* 19 (1903): 226–63.

sense, seeks to attract men and betrays perverse homosexual inclinations, and if when the mistake in sex is discovered he energetically opposes every attempt to make him abandon girls' petticoats, their way of life, and his feminine predilections and occupations, and if he declines to assume male attire and change his social position, and appear in future as a man. Such homosexual inclinations acquired by suggestion have in some cases been only temporary, and the male, though brought up by mistake as a female, has, sooner or later, recognized his virility, and has not hesitated to demand his social and sexual rights sometimes somewhat abruptly. There have been instances in which a male person, recognizing that his true sexual position had been misunderstood, has adopted male attire without consulting anyone, and without giving notice of the fact to the magistrate or any other authority; one such person found a mistress whom he put in the family way, and only demanded the adjustment of his social position on the evidence of that pregnancy—an incontestable proof of his manhood. In other cases the genetic sense with homosexual desire has persisted during the whole life of an hermaphrodite, whose true sex has been misunderstood; there have even been instances in which hermaphrodites of the male sex brought up as girls, have, then, too late, their true sex has been recognized, with all possible insistence demanded castration.

But this can lead to a sense of alienation if one does not resolve the question of sexual identity:

The consciousness of being neither man nor woman, the constant and shameful fear that the malformation, though concealed with the utmost care, may some day betray itself and leave the sufferer to be the scorn and derision of those about him, are perpetually upsetting the mental balance and psychotic repose of the unfortunate pseudohermaphrodite, who racks his brain demanding why he should be so afflicted, and seeking some way out of his miserable social position. Not daring to confide in anyone the poor hybrid passes his days and nights dwelling upon his lot; feeling excluded from the society of either men or women he cultivates solitude and avoids intimacy of any kind with anyone; he passes his nights in agony and tears; his health gives way, and he becomes suspicious, distrustful, shy, savage, irritable, irascible, vindictive, violent, and impulsive to an extent that may drive him to crime, or he becomes moody, apathetic, and melancholy, till at last he ends his days in self-destruction.

In Imperial Berlin, male cross-dressers could be arrested just because they appeared different. In Weimar Germany, such cross-dressers (not necessarily homosexuals or hermaphrodites) were given identity cards to allow them to present themselves in public. Such a social danger of mis-seeing haunted the world in which Baer grew up. What would happen if one looked inappropriate for one's sex?

On December 2, 1891, a gendarme arrested a young girl of 19 on the platform of the railway station at Pilsen, on the suspicion of being a man disguised as a woman. It was in vain that the prisoner showed her personal papers, in which she was described as Marie Karfiol, born on such a day, at such place, and of such parents. In spite of her protestations, she was taken to the mayor's court, where medical evidence proved that there had been an error of sex, and that Marie K. was a male hypospadiac. She then admitted that at the time of her birth there had been some difficulty in determining her sex, but she had been brought up as a girl. At the time of her puberty suspicions as to the real state of the case had led to her being taken to see the mayor of her village and the priest; but no further action had been taken. Later on she abandoned herself to her fate, being ashamed to speak to anyone of her doubts. Her pretty hair was cut off and she was dressed in men's clothes; but in her novel attire she had a very timid and wild appearance.

Thus the anxiety focused on the feminized appearance of the male. This runs like a red thread through Baer's autobiography. His female schoolmates will not play with him because their teachers call him a boy; equally telling is the fact that "street urchins also shouted 'Norbert' after me": he was seen as "something odd" in public. When the older Baer loses his passport on a trip to Hungary as a newspaper correspondent, the police see "her" as a disguised man, which is "very suspicious." It is only the fact that a passerby recognizes her from her portrait in a women's magazine that rescues Baer. Being seen as different on the street was dangerous, especially if the assumption was that you were a feminized man.

Cesare Taruffi's classic monograph on hermaphrodism, originally published in Italian in 1902, appeared in 1903 in Germany. Here the notion that Hirschfeld had stressed—of the hermaphrodite as model case—was spelled out in explicit detail. The model is always the feminization of the male as an answer to sexual dimorphism and sexual identity. Baer's life as he recounts it after his transformation is that of a feminized man, not that of a mannish woman. Feminization is here to be understood both in its general, cultural sense and in its specifically medical sense. Feminization, or the existence of the "feminized man," is a form of "external pseudo-hermaphrodism."[16] It is not true hermaphrodism but rather the sharing of external, secondary sexual characteristics, such as the shape of the body or the tone of the voice. The concept begins in the middle of the nineteenth century with the introduction of the term *infemminsce*, to feminize, to describe the supposed results of the castration of the male.[17] By the 1870s, the term was used to describe the *feminisme* of the male through the effects of other diseases, such as tuberculosis.[18] Here is Baer's fantasy that the dropping of his voice was a sign of tuberculosis, as "consumptives are often hoarse." One can see him reading in the medical (or popular medical) literature of the day, looking for a pathology that would explain his growing masculinization. He "coughed, suffered from backaches" and "in [his] lively imagination thought [he] felt all the symptoms mentioned in the book." Indeed, he later uses a feigned case of "consumption" to return home from his first job, as an apprentice in a banking house, "as my lungs had become weak." But what he was doing was simply reversing the model: diseases such as tuberculosis feminized men, according to the literature of the time, precisely the problem from which he actually suffered. He has a need to see his state as an expression of a somatic pathology but one that could be treated. Feminization was the direct result of actual castration or the physiological

16. Cesare Taruffi, *Hermaphrodismus und Zeugungsunfähigkeit: Eine systematische Darstellung des Missbildungen der menschlichen Geschlechtsorgane*, trans. R. Teuscher (Berlin: H. Barsdorf, 1903), pp. 96–103.

17. Ibid., p. 97.

18. Ferdinand-Valére Faneau de la Cour, *Du féminisme et de l'infantilisme chez les tuberculeux* (Paris: A. Parent, 1871).

equivalent, such as an intensely debilitating illness. It reshaped the body.

Baer's autobiography is remarkable as much for its mode of masking its subject's identity as it is for its candor. But Baer does something unique. He redefines his ancestry as "French" in order to explain his social difference: "Our lineage is not German. Our forefathers came from France. My family is very old and proud of its family tree, whose beginnings reach back as far as the sixteenth century. For generations, however, the descendants of this old family had moved up to the heights of existence, only to soon descend to the middling life of small shopkeepers."

"French" was viewed in Baer's time as a racial category as well as a political one. Thus the arch-racist French count Joseph Arthur de Gobineau (1816–82), widely read in Germany, argued the inherent superiority of the "Aryans" (Germans) over the "Celts" (French). Being French in Germany is a racial label that is mirrored in the body: "Our outward appearance alone is enough to easily distinguish us from the other inhabitants of Bergheim: black or brown eyes, brown wavy hair, and sharply defined southern European features are seldom found among the Saxons and Franconians of those mountain valleys." These "French" bodies seem to be just as visible as the odd masculine body of the hermaphrodite.

Baer's French mask is transparent but is also unnecessary, as there is no reason in the argument of his autobiography for his identity to be anything but that of a hermaphrodite. It is the "somber gray [that] hung over our path through life." Yet there was clearly a need to stress another category of difference that also affected his understanding of his own body. As Hermann Simon has brilliantly shown in his detective work that identifies Baer as the author of N. O. Body's autobiography, Baer was not only a Jew but was also able to create a meaningful life for himself as an officer of the Berlin lodges of the Jewish fraternal organization of the B'nai B'rith (Brothers of the Circumcision). That group seemed to have demanded neither educational certification nor birth records, as Baer fears at the end of his account. His absence of any formal education as male meant that his social role was truly damaged. He stresses this himself. It was sufficient for them that he was a member of the Jewish community.

It is also the case that being Jewish and living uncomfortably as a woman has evident parallels in Baer's self, at least in 1907. The volume is prefaced by an anonymous poem:

Over my childhood
Hung a threatening fist.
All my peaceful pleasures
Were shrouded in a mist.

The wounds this left were deep,
Like a dagger, stabbing me,
I could forget them, or dream them away . . .
But healed—they never shall be.

As the reader's introduction to the struggles of Martha's learning to be a young woman, this poem reflects the author's sense of a trauma beyond healing. Repression perhaps; but reconstitution never. Baer borrows (and very slightly adapts) the text from his Zionist friend Theodor Zlocisti's *About the Path Home: Verses of a Jew (Vom Heimweg: Verse eines Juden)* (1903).[19] There the lines clearly refer to the actual author's Jewish identity in the Diaspora. The transformation of the politics of a fixed German Jewish identity into the politics of sexual identity leaves the "wound" unstated. Perhaps both indeed are present.

Baer becomes French rather than Jewish in his account in 1907 because the sexual implications of being Jewish are clear to him. Just as he transforms all of the Jewish holidays and practices into Catholic ones in his account of his early life, as Simon shows, so does he desire to transform his Jewish body into a French one. (Being Catholic in late nineteenth-century Berlin at the time of the *Kulturkampf* against the Vatican was almost as exotic as being Jewish.) That the Jew was

19. Hermann Simon, "N. O. Body und kein Ende," in Marion Kaplan and Beate Meyer, eds., *Jüdische Welten: Juden in Deutschland vom 18. Jahrhundert bis in die Gegenwart* (Göttingen: Wallstein, 2005), pp. 225–30.

an anomalous sexual case was part of his world. For Baer and for the world in which he loved, the "damaged" genitalia of the male Jew, damaged through circumcision—though there is a debate as to whether circumcision can be inherited after generations—meant that the male Jew is already neither truly male nor actually female. He becomes, to use Ulrichs's coinage, "a third sex."

It is clear that the model that Ulrichs employed to characterize the homosexual as beyond the dimorphism of traditional sexual identity is analogous to the argument that Theodor Herzl used to establish Zionism. If the Jews were inherently "oriental," the basic argument in the Berlin anti-Semitism struggle of the 1880s, then the Jews should recognize their "oriental" nature, leave Europe, and return to Palestine. It is not a blemish but a recognition of their natural state. Being different in both cases is transformed from a pathological and stigmatizing identity to a positive one.

It is in the physiology of the male Jew that the myth of Jewish sexual difference is located. Circumcision, however, is not a powerful enough myth; the world of European anti-Semitism creates the notion that male Jews menstruate. Menstruation is the sign of womanhood in Baer's autobiography. It is "a dark matter," as it had to do with "sexuality, and because one was then an adult." All of the girls in Baer's school "were 'it' already," so Baer, too, "arrived at school one morning, beaming. 'It' was there." This "lie" continued for "ten years, in many countries and among strange customs, and it caused me many a worry." Doubly so, for had Baer read further into nineteenth-century medical literature on the topic of male menstruation, by writers such as F. A. Forel and W. D. Halliburton, he would have found a fascination with male menstruation with regard to the problem of hermaphroditism as a sign of bisexuality as prominent in the nineteenth century.[20] Paul Albrecht in Hamburg argued for the existence of "male menstruation,"

20. See, for example, F. A. Forel, "Cas de menstruation chez un homme," *Bulletin de la Societé médicale de la Suisse romande* (Lausanne, 1869): 53–61; and W. D. Halliburton, "A Peculiar Case," *Weekly Medical Review and Journal of Obstetrics* (St. Louis, 1885): 392.

which was periodic and which mimicked the menstrual cycle of the female through the release of white corpuscles into the urine.[21] The sexologist Paul Näcke provided a detailed discussion of the question of "male menstruation" and its relationship to the problem of male periodicity.[22] Näcke cited, among others, Havelock Ellis, who had been collecting material on this question for years. With the rise of modern sexology at the close of the nineteenth century, especially in the writings of Magnus Hirschfeld, male menstruation came to hold a very special place in the "proofs" for the continuum between male and female sexuality.[23] The hermaphrodite, the male who was believed to menstruate, became a central focus of Hirschfeld's work. But all of this new "science" that used the existence of male menstruation still drew on the image of the marginality of those males who menstruated and thus pointed toward a much more ancient tradition.

The idea of male menstruation is part of a Christian tradition of seeing the Jew as inherently, biologically different. From the late fourth-century *Adversus Judaeos* (Against the Jews) of the early church father Saint John Chrysostom through the work of Thomas Cantipratanus, the thirteenth-century anatomist, the abnormal and abhorrent body of the Jew marked the implacable difference of Jewish males. The argument was that male Jews menstruated as a mark of the "Father's curse," their pathological difference.[24] This view continued throughout the Middle Ages until the early modern period. The view that attributed to the Jews diseases for which the "sole cure was Christian blood" reappeared again as part of the blood-libel accusations in the

21. Paolo Albrecht, "Sulla Mestruazione ne maschio," *L'Anomalo* 2 (1880): 33.

22. Paul Näcke, "Kritisches zum Kapitel der normalen und pathologischen Sexualität," *Archiv für Psychiatrie und Nervenkrankheiten* 32 (1899): 356–86, here, 364–65.

23. Hirschfeld, *Sexualpathologie*, 2:1–92.

24. Thomas de Cantimpré, *Miraculorum et exemplorum memorabilium sui temporis libro duo* (Duaci: Baltazris Belleri, 1605), pp. 305–6.

late nineteenth century.[25] It was raised again at the turn of the century in a powerfully written pamphlet by a professor of Hebrew at the University in Saint Petersburg, Daniel Chwolson, as one of the rationales used to justify the blood libel, that Jews killed Christian children (or virgins) to cure themselves. Chwolson notes that it was used to "cure the diseases believed to be specifically those of the Jews," such as male menstruation.[26] This version of the blood accusation ties the meaning of the form of the circumcised genitalia to the Jew's diseased nature.

These older charges about Jewish male menstruation, of Jewish hermaphrodism, reappear with their reprinting in the nineteenth century.[27] By the end of the nineteenth century, the arch-racist Theodor Fritsch—whose *Anti-Semite's Catechism*, first published in 1887, was the encyclopedia of German anti-Semitism—saw the sexuality of the Jew as inherently different from that of the German: "The Jew has a different sexuality from the Teuton; he will [not] and cannot understand it. And if he attempts to understand it, then the destruction of the German soul can result."[28] The hidden sign that the Jewish man is neither male nor female is his menstruation. The implicit charge of pathological bisexuality, of hermaphrodism, had traditionally been lodged against the Jewish male. (Male Jews are like women because, among other things, they both menstruate as a sign of their pathological difference.)

But Baer was a Jewish girl who did not menstruate but had to maintain the fantasy that he did. Was he, as he presumed in his first

25. Anatole Leroy-Beaulieu, *Israël chez les nations: Les Juifs et l'antisémitisme* (Paris: Calmann Lévy, 1893), pp. 166–67.

26. Daniel Chwolson, *Die Blutanklage und sonstige mittelalterliche Beschuldigungen der Juden: Eine historische Untersuchung nach den Quellen* (Frankfurt am Main: J. Kauffmann, 1901), pp. 7, 207–10.

27. Chrysostomus Dudulaelus, *Gründliche und Warhafftige Relation von einem Juden auss Jerusalem mit Nahmen Ahassverus* (n.p.: n.p., [1602]), p. Diiir; reprinted as *Evangelischer Bericht vom den Leben Jesu Christi . . .* (Stuttgart: J. Scheible, 1856), p. 126.

28. Theodor Fritsch, *Handbuch der Judenfrage* (Leipzig: Hammer, 1935), p. 409.

real job, merely an "anemic and poorly developed" girl, for whom "menstruation did not begin before the twenties"? Or was he truly different? The question of ritual cleanliness during and after menstruation, the identification of his body as the antithesis of the menstruating Jewish male—here, the female who does not menstruate—is clarified only when he comes to understand his body as that of a healthy, Jewish male, who does not menstruate. Masculinity, like Jewishness, will out. The resolution of Baer's conflict comes through a physician who recognizes him as a man and urges him to comprehend his desire for a woman as "a natural feeling." All ambiguities are resolved, Baer claims, and the state resolves his question of identity by reassigning him as a man. He trains his new male body through exercise and sport. He becomes a "real" man except for "a slight furrow left behind from tight lacing." That mark remains written on the body. No circumcision marked Baer's new male body but the scar of his role as a woman. Yet the world in which he remade himself was the world of a growing anti-Semitism in which the appearance of the Jew on the street was as clearly marked as that of the woman. Indeed, the closing of the public clinic for cosmetic surgery in Nazi Germany (in 1933) and the introduction of the yellow star (in 1942; 1939 in Poland) were both aimed at making the invisible visible, as the fabled ability to recognize Jews at a glance turned out to be an anti-Semitic fantasy. Baer ends his life in Israel after his flight to Palestine from Germany in 1938. By then, Germany was more obsessed by Jews than by the ambiguity of gender.

Memoirs of a Man's Maiden Years

Foreword

RUDOLF PRESBER

I have been asked to write a short preface to this strange book, which contains an account only of things that have been experienced and nothing that has been invented. I cannot take it upon myself to speak in a substantial manner to the vital questions this book raises for parents and educators in need of guidance. Rather, I write here for the simple reason that this book was written in the first place because of me. I was the first to point out to a human being, worried about his future, that he might be able to assist many people with hidden sorrows and help solve many a disastrous riddle among the misunderstood tragedies of everyday life if he would reveal his youthful fate honestly, without even a hint of sensationalism. I suggested that a young person of his ability, a person who had been uprooted by his strange fate and isolated by the inhibitions of the proper, the fortunate, and the normal, might find a purpose in his new, undreamed-of circumstances, and thus serenity for his frightened heart and self-confidence for his confused character.

A doctor with whom I had literary matters to discuss came to visit me and brought with him a young woman. She was slender, flat-chested, with strong, slightly reddish hands, and a strange, harsh, and deep voice. But in dress, movement, and manner of expressing herself, she was a well-brought-up young lady. Seeing her in the street or on a train, I would perhaps have taken her for a language teacher or a student, and her lively and intelligent conversation would certainly have supported this assumption. Astounded, I listened to the story of her life, which she related in simple words, without pathos or the harshness of accusation, but with the subdued pain caused by an oppressive youth. Only occasionally did the doctor add a word or two of explanation to the strange account of this unusual life.

In my home, all the names and facts were disclosed, which in this book have had to be concealed out of discretion and out of consideration for the living and the dead who erred, and because of the young person's understandable shyness before the embarrassing curiosity of the masses. I gained the impression that a nasty whim of nature, in conjunction with humanity enslaved by custom, tradition, and fear of ridicule and disgrace, had created one of those novels that winds its way from comedy to tragedy, but a novel, the precise likes of which no imaginative author has ever dared invent. At the end of a joyless youth, half suffocated under the veil of secrecy, had come a defiant battle for human rights, a hard struggle to achieve the admission of old grave errors, a fatiguing war with the law, which does not understand miracles and begrudges the (seemingly) unique its rights, now and in the future, and allows it no refuge.

Two weeks later, the same visitor, and yet *not* the same: in place of the young woman, a young man. Her twin brother, from a Shakespearean comedy, which in its boisterousness borders on the unlikely. The same facial features, the figure, hands, and feet, all the same. But the full head of hair, formerly pinned up, had now been cut short and was brushed in a man's style. The steps in men's trousers were still short and somewhat tentative. The movements were slightly forced in their boyishness, as if every minute they were angrily attempting to cast aside the constraints of two decades that had been unwillingly borne by nature. What in the girl of bygone days had perhaps been somewhat too hard and masculine for an eye searching for grace and femininity appeared in this still somewhat immature youth rather too soft and feminine. The sexes are mixed in him, as though this person, who does not conform to normal standards, is destined to kindle suspicion of a cunning masquerade and to provoke doubts about his genuineness, no matter in which sex's garb he appears.

Encouraged by my friendly interest, which is far removed from mere titillated curiosity, "he" takes up the thread of his story, more and more answering to himself rather than telling me all the peculiar things connected with his struggle for his rights. Again and again, into his honest words there creeps the quiet fear of: What now? Where is the path to a new life for the transformed person, the path to work, to responsibilities, to a livelihood? Then the thought occurs to me: Why is he telling this to *me* alone? To me, who can marvel at the story as something never before heard, who is separated by worlds from these experiences and this fate? Why does he not tell it to *everyone*, in simple and calm words, as he has told it to me, so that it will reach those who may be responsible for terrible mistakes in child rearing? To those, too, who, standing at the gravesides of youths who have killed themselves, find the reasons for the last irreparable step merely in the suicides' poor grades, or their fear of punishment, or their momentary mental confusion?

What is new and unnatural does not become good, gentle, and benign by our failing to look at it directly. And what is supposedly repulsive, on which we perfectly normal people like to turn our backs as on something unclean, will not disappear from the earth because we deny its existence. Above all, the physical and mental health of humanity has never profited from hypocrisy.

This is approximately what I told the intelligent young man who, only a fortnight before, had been, in the eyes of the state and society, a young woman. I also told him, "If you wish to begin a new life, give yourself and others an account of what lies behind you, calmly and without dragging the delicate matter onto the garish stage of sensationalism. Write it down exactly as you have told it to me. Do not fill in the gaps in your memory with arbitrary figments of your imagination, and do not present yourself with vanity, as the hero of an incredible novel. Do not preach, and do not attack. Just say: this is how my life was. And with every honest line you write, a rusty fetter that cuts into your flesh, a sad piece of the past that oppresses you will fall away. And on the path of this first task that you perform as a *man*, you may find your way to a new profession, a new lifelong purpose, for which you are now searching, hemmed in by all the strangeness, the un-accustomed and embarrassing things, still timid and without proper confidence."

Thus, he decided to write this book. At the beginning, he asked a few questions, groped his way toward the proper form to convey what he wished to say. Then I heard nothing further from him until I saw the printed galleys.

Everything that appears on these pages is exactly as I heard it when, in his head—which had just been freed of women's hair—there was *no* thought of paper and printing ink, no wish to make a book out of the struggle and suffering that had been overcome.

It seemed to be my duty to say this here, for on account of the anonymity of the young person who suffered through and wrote this book, his readers have no other way of verifying the story.

Spring 1907

Over my childhood
Hung a threatening fist.
All my peaceful pleasures
Were shrouded in a mist.

The wounds this left were deep,
Like a dagger, stabbing me,
I could forget them, or dream them away . . .
But healed—they never shall be.

This book tells a true story. In it, what was probably the strangest youth ever lived, shall speak with its own voice. This life needs to be believed, as strange as it may seem. But strangeness need not be equated with lies. In this book, I wish to speak of a life that lay like a burden on an obscure human being until a woman's soft white hands lifted the weight from him and transformed his sorrow into joie de vivre. It is the story of the confusion and conflicts that arose for me from my very own nature.

I was born a boy, raised as a girl. The fabric of my life was twisted from tangled threads until, with a mighty blow, the inner nature of my masculinity tore apart the veil of half-truths that upbringing, habit, and vital necessity had spun about me. One may raise a healthy boy in as womanish a manner as one wishes, and a female creature in as mannish; never will this cause their senses to remain forever reversed. But customs and habits bind so tightly that it needed an impulse from without, which was, however, also felt strongly from within, before I resolved to undertake the decisive outer transformation.

And the decision fell when a woman entered my life. I also wish to speak here of the love of this woman, who cleared the thorns from my path and transformed my life which had been nothing but dark torment into a joyous blessing.

My entire life was a path filled with thorns, until, finally, I reached her.

Rain in May, make me big!
I am so terribly tiny,
Please make me shiny!
Yoho!

The cheerful melody of this nursery rhyme is the first sound that echoes through my conscious life from the dark land of earliest memory. My memory reaches back to my third year. From that time comes a scene that stands as clearly before my eyes as if I had seen myself in it only yesterday.

A May morning in my small hometown. A rain shower had driven people from the streets. The last drops are still falling, but people are beginning to appear again. The sky still looks sullen, but to make up for this, the sun has painted a beautiful rainbow onto the gray. And in the spray of those last shining colored raindrops, lit up by the May sunshine, a crowd of children are playing. Little girls are singing a song with shrill voices. They are playing in front of a large gray building, at whose gate an old fountain is splashing its waters into a plain stone basin. All the children are merry and cheerful, except one who is standing to one side beside the rain gutter, like a wild boy, letting the falling water wash over her boots. Her glance wanders over to the little girls, half longingly, half defiantly, as if she does not dare join the game, uninvited. When no one calls to her to join them, her little foot stamps in the puddle so that the water splashes up high. Now the other children come running and gather around this little girl, this child is wearing girls' clothing in any case, and shout, "Boy, boy, bad boy!" The startled child then runs into the house, crying.

That child was me. It was so long ago, and yet the burning pain and childish defiance still resound within me when I recall this scene.

I was born on Whitsunday in 1884. A Sunday child. My parents were well educated and, at that time, well-off. I am the youngest child. When they were very young, three siblings fell victim to an epidemic children's disease. My mother, who at that time was a month from giving birth to my brother, had to part with three hitherto healthy children in a single week. She was twenty-two years old on the day of her marriage, and forty when I was born; my father was six years older. I resemble neither of them, but generally favor my paternal family: fine limbs, long slender feet, and a longish, oval face.

I know nothing of the time before my birth, but of my birth, I have been told that it proceeded normally. The midwife congratulated my mother on the birth of a splendid little girl and then called my father, to whom she said that the physical properties of the newborn were so strange that she was unable to decide to which sex the child belonged. She assumed it was a girl.

My father, too, inclined toward this view, whereas my mother wished to raise her child as a boy. They decided to consult a doctor. The family doctor we had then was an excellent man, however, anything but a doctor. "On superficial inspection, the shape has a feminine appearance; ergo we have a girl before us," he summarily decreed.

My mother raised several objections and wished to consult a leading medical authority; however, she was overridden, and my sanguine father put her off until some time in the future. His main worry had been to make sure that the doctor (by means of a handshake) and the midwife (by means of a large sum of money) would keep silent, so that this "dreadfully disagreeable thing" should not become known in wider circles. With that, his interest was exhausted; the unhappy child would have to get through life as best it could.

Altogether, my birth caused little joy. My father found me, whom he later called a living reproach, unpleasant. My nine-year-old brother, Hans, thought me a bawling brat. The love of my oldest sister, too, soon came to an end. Because of my tiny size, she had taken me for one of those large dolls that can say "papa" and "mama" when squeezed. When she made the unpleasant discovery that the tiny thing only screamed when squeezed, just an ordinary scream, and said neither "papa" nor "mama" nor anything else, she returned to her other toys.

My other sister, a speculative four-year-old mathematical wizard, was quite dissatisfied; "I am not the youngest anymore now, and the new one will always get the sweets!"

The first years of my life proceeded normally. I have retained only one image from that period, a fleeting flash of memory. I must have been very small when a big blond woman took off my little nightdress, joking all the while, and placed me into a tub. But I saw that, despite her cheerful words, tears came to her eyes. Then I was taken into a dark cave with a golden star, which cast its rays onto my little bed.

Today I understand the image, which long remained in my memory. It was my mother who undressed me, and the golden star was the night lamp, whose glow shed only a weak light in the large bedroom.

Since I have learned to forget the resentment that I felt toward my parents for so long, I can now understand what my mother suffered. I feel for the woman who was moved to tears by the sight of her child's body.

I spent my childhood years in Saxony, in the small royal summer seat of Bergheim. I ask you not to attempt to look for it on any map, for no one will find it under that name among the colorful specks of land that make up our dear Saxony-Thuringia and that stand out so brightly and cheerfully from gray Prussia that every schoolchild delights in them.

The town lies tranquilly, forgotten by the world, between two mountains, from one of which a castle, now lying in ruins, looks down on the valley.

The house where I was born had been the property of my family for many years. Its large building is part of an old monastery and once belonged to a duke. It consists of two low stories and an attic under tall gables. Because it is built of gray sandstone, people called it the gray court, and a shadow of the monotonous gray of its walls hung over the souls of all who were born in that house. A dull gray veil always lay over the nooks and crannies, and on dark days in the winter, the lamps were not switched off at all.

The front of the building stood on the marketplace, the facade facing the north, so that a sunbeam seldom shone into the large but low rooms. The wide entrance hall was furnished with tall oak cupboards, and from the corridor a steep staircase led to the bedrooms. The first room on the right was my parents' bedroom, and adjoining it was my brother's study. To the left lay my sisters' bedroom, and next to it lay mine. Like the others, it made a gloomy impression.

A few pretty doilies and some bright curtains would have sufficed to change my somber, cheerless room into a pleasant, friendly place. But then it would not have been in harmony with the other rooms in the gray house, where anything bright and cheerful was excluded.

But I do not wish to be bitter and unjust, for it was this very room that witnessed the few cheerful hours that my childhood provided.

The darkest room in our gloomy house was our dining room. It was a large, broad hall that received murky light through two small windows that lay in deep niches. On rainy days, it was so dark there that one could barely see one's plate during the midday meal.

In the three centuries since the dissolution of the old monastery, the successive owners had made many changes to the old building, so that of the actual monastery buildings, nothing more than the outer walls remained. A second flight of stairs led down to the courtyard, which served as a storage yard for the timber trade, in which my father engaged.

The lofts above the storehouses built around the courtyard were considered to be in a bad state of repair and mostly lay unused. We children were strictly forbidden to enter them during our games. This rule did little good, however, for the lofts, in their mysterious semi-darkness, attracted us time and again.

Roaming about up there was just too glorious. We could feel like masters there, because no adult liked to trust his bones to those unsteady floorboards. When the swirling dust that we kicked up with our feet took our breath away, a creepy feeling came over us so that we dared not speak. Here and there, a board in the rotting floor would crack, and one had to leap aside quickly to avoid the danger of breaking through. Every step was bound up with minor perils, which my vivid imagination enlarged into horrors. Best of all was the pleasant consciousness of treading forbidden paths! But it was particular fun when we discovered a forgotten old box in a corner. We would creep up to it cautiously and beat on the thing, using the long sticks with which we had armed ourselves down below in the wood yard. Sometimes, an enemy really did leap out at us, a marten or a cat, or a frightened squeaking would reveal that a group of mice had been startled from their peace and were now fleeing to safety.

We felt the greatest dread one day when we discovered the "bricked-up cell with the bones." I was about nine at the time. My two friends Hans and Leo, two children who lived in the neighborhood, and I had just read a bloodcurdling tale about a monk who had been punished by being immured alive and whose bleached bones were discovered years later by "the lovely damsel who had found his favor." We thought this damsel must be some kind of "auntie."

Still under the sway of this hair-raising tale, we embarked together on an expedition through the loft. We had not rummaged around for long when we came upon a large box whose lid gave way under Leo's foot. Horror and dismay! Bones lay within! Hans, a delicate, nervous boy whom I never took seriously because of his girlishness, threw a screaming fit. More dead than alive, we arrived downstairs with the howling boy. The end of our expedition, which we had begun with such high hopes, was equally pathetic and humiliating for us three heroes: each of us received a terrible thrashing, and the nursemaid who had stashed the bones away up there, not monk's bones, but oxen bones, in order to sell them, was dismissed.

Despite that experience, those lofts remained our childhood paradise. The courtyard was vast and light. Out there, one felt nothing of the musty, oppressive air of the house. A fresh fragrance of fir resin or the tangy smell of wilting oak leaves filled the wood yard.

How I loved the courtyard, the only bright place in my family home. When the wagons, heavily laden with timber, drove in, and the huge tree trunks rose and fell, I heard through their groaning the woe of farewell from the great forest, and the drops of resin pouring forth from them seemed to me like tears shed for their lost youth. In front of the house stood the fountain I mentioned before, the murmur of which sounded gently in those childhood dreams. A strange figure decorated it or rather, disfigured it. Its head was missing; the head had fallen down one day with a loud thud and lay there for many years in our yard, deeply embedded in the soft clay. This head, like the fountain, played an important role in my imagination.

In later years, I have often thought of this house and its grave character when I read Ibsen's *Rosmerholm*, the book about the children who are unable to laugh. That is how our house was, too. A somber gray hung over our path through life, like tedious days filled with worries. The house gave me a portion of its own unhappy, joyless existence to carry with me; otherwise, my life would surely not have been so wretched.

Our lineage is not German. Our forefathers came from France. My family is very old and proud of its family tree, whose beginnings reach back as far as the sixteenth century. For generations, however, the descendants of this old family had moved up to the heights of existence, only to soon descend to the middling life of small shopkeepers. But in them all lived the strong belief that one day their trunk would once more lift its branches up to the light. And this belief casts some light on their dark paths. We trace our lineage back to a Franciscan monk who left his order at the time of the Reformation and founded a family. His grandchildren ended up in the mountain town in Saxony and settled there. Our outward appearance alone is enough to distinguish us from the other inhabitants of Bergheim: black or brown eyes, brown wavy hair, and sharply defined southern European features are seldom found among the Saxons and Franconians of those mountain valleys. Our racial type is so sharply defined because my family hardly mixed with their fellow citizens and kept their blood fairly pure by means of numerous marriages between relatives. In each of our souls, a glimmer of the blue French sky lives on, a wondrous contrast to the shadows that the gray house cast over us.

I can still remember my paternal grandfather, Ernst, a white-haired old gentleman with the chivalrous courtesy of bygone days. As a child growing up, I particularly admired him for the romantic manner in which he had won his wife, my grandmother Anna.

Anna was a cousin, and because there had already been several marriages between relatives in the family, both sets of parents refused to give their consent to the marriage. The lovers appeared to accept their fate, and instead of losing heart, Anna turned with more enthusiasm than before to housekeeping. She even did the shopping for the large household at dusk, after she had completed her day's work. And Cousin Ernst suddenly found that his father's horses had too little exercise, so he would ride one of them for a stretch to the next village every evening.

One evening, they both failed to return. The old servant, Lene, who had been Anna's wet nurse, had disappeared from the house as well. The next morning, a messenger on horseback delivered a letter, which said that all three had found refuge with friends and were only prepared to return under the condition that parental approval be given to Anna and Ernst's marriage. After that, their parents had to give their blessing.

By the way, most members of my family wooed with considerable passion. Of my mother's family, I know little or nothing that may have influenced the course of my life. They were all healthy long-lived people, without physical abnormalities or mental peculiarities. On my father's side, too, I know of no cases of mental or physical degeneration. I only know that hot blood and a short life span were the general rule. These ancestors had a zest for life, like a fear of being called away too early from laden tables. All these men followed their paths determinedly. They seemed hard and unapproachable only because they kept their loves and longings deeply hidden, permitting only a few to look into their souls.

I have not much to say about my parents. Outwardly, my father appeared sunny and pleasant to all, but at home he succumbed easily to unbridled rage. My mother is a fine, kind woman. My father, who has been dead for a long time, was the victim of a painful disease during the last ten years of his life and was confined to a wheelchair. In his dealings with the outside world, he bore his affliction like a hero; but only we, the people around him, know how his family suffered under his violent temper. During his entire illness, my father was nursed with complete devotion by my mother. I cannot judge whether love outweighed a sense of duty, or vice versa.

During all those years, a dull pressure, which kept pleasure and joy from our childhood, lay over our lives. Before my birth, my family was considered wealthy. My father had inherited a good business, and my mother had brought a substantial fortune into the marriage. But the conditions, and perhaps a lack of understanding of the requirements of the times, had led to a decline in the business, which was, after all, only a small one. At the time of my birth, I do not think our fortune exceeded twenty thousand marks. Of course, our landed property was worth far more but was overburdened by mortgages. One day when I was a small child, my father spoke to my mother of the difficulties of accommodating another "mortgage"; our roof could not bear a further burden. For days, I wandered about with my head down, looking for a corner where that thing with the dreadful name could be accommodated.

Because of this falsely placed interest in my father's financial affairs, I once incurred severe punishment. I was so engrossed in the problem of what the thing with the dreadful name really meant that I asked a friend of my father's about it, the town clergyman, in whose sagacity I had the greatest confidence. Of course, I asked him when we were undisturbed, for it seemed to me that Papa was not particularly fond of this subject, that I found so very interesting. Therefore, I asked the clergyman what those things with the strange name were, the things that were sometimes placed on the roof. Unfortunately, the good gentleman did not understand me at first, and so I explained that Papa had said to Mama that there were already so many of them lying on our roof that there was no room for any more. But instead of answering, the gentleman laughed at me, and clumsily, as adults often are when they enter the narrow paths of children's territory, he was still laughing when Papa entered the room. As a result of his amusement, I received an undeserved thrashing.

After this description of my environment, I must return to the beginnings of my development. And there I find myself again at about the age of four.

Three children dressed in girls' clothing are sitting beneath a tree. It was a tall elder tree, under which we liked to play. The leafy tree protected us from the sun and at the same time from unwanted eyes during our games. The two little girls were Hilde and Lene, my two neighborhood friends, one of whom was about four weeks younger, the other three months older than I was. At this time, the gates to our courtyard were not yet open to me, and my world was confined to the house and the garden in which we were playing. Later, when I was permitted to go out on my own into the street, I no longer played with girls very often. They were too gentle for me, and my boisterous, wild nature was ill-suited to their quiet games.

That tree no longer stands there. When I visited my hometown a short while ago in order to see the sites of my childhood once again, I searched for the elder tree. But it had been chopped down when its dead branches no longer provided any shade. In its place, over the bench that was still standing on the same spot, a gazebo covered in Virginia creeper had been erected.

This seemed to be an allegory about life: one goes forth to search for the blooming bushes of childhood and finds autumnal creeper growing rampant where one left behind blooming roses. Fortunate is he who is able to take delight in the blaze of color of the leaves when he has overcome his disappointment. However, many set forth in search of roses and forget that winter has set in. It is those people whose souls bleed when they search for their childhood. The wind has caused the rose to shed its petals, and those people grasp at thorns.

In those days, we took pleasure in the shade of our tree. We sat languidly on the bench. In front of us was a heap of sand upon which wooden sand molds were scattered.

It must have been spring, because the sweet fragrance of blooming elder trees filled the garden. When the wind blew gently through the trees, it carried blossoms down to us, which lay like snow on our hair. The deep blue sky peeked through the bunches of white blossoms. Nearby, nimble swallows performed their graceful love play.

The soporific peacefulness of nature fatigued me. Drunk with sleep, I laid my head on Hilde's shoulder. Quietly, she let me slip onto her lap. With sweet earnestness, she began to stroke my face and neck. I submitted to this pleasure contentedly. Then she roughly pushed away the other little girl and occupied her place as well; she half threw herself over me, kissing my mouth and hair. It was a fantastic game. And over it all the laughing blue sky, fragrant elder blossoms, and the love songs of the swallows. Delphiniums and fritillarias shone from the flower beds.

Sleepily, we closed our eyes. Hilde's kisses became wilder than ever.

I think I felt somewhat surprised at such passion. She snuggled up to me; her hands wandered over my dress, and, as if in a dream, I felt the buttons and ribbons coming undone and the hot little hands caressing my body. Lene watched this game, wide-eyed.

The sun shone hotly on our faces. We woke up for a moment, looking around for shade. The old elder tree stretched out its branches to us protectively. We crept into the deepest shade of its leaves, where we moved close together and let our hands wander to one another. I still recall that we felt no revulsion for one another's bodies, although we had been taught to do so by our mothers. Dizzy and hot from the excitement of our new game, we remained crouched in the sand for a while, entirely covered by the blooming branches. Every involuntary movement caused the white, star-shaped blossoms to drift down upon us, and the touch of them brought about a strange feeling of pleasure. And still, the hands continued to search, grope, and caress, until the dinner bell was rung in the wood yard. We sprang apart for a moment, only to press even closer together afterward.

How long this lasted, I do not know. Later, the tension eased somewhat. The hands rested from their nervous haste, and our eyes began to search, searching and peeking, looking again and again, and comparing what the little hands had previously been so eagerly searching for. I recall what the two little girls said and can still hear the surprised sound of their voices. "Look here, Nora is very different from us." We compared once again; this gave occasion for renewed touching, but the disconcerting fact remained unchanged.

I am puzzled by the fact that the games were able to remain so harmless. In any case, from then on I was the darling of the two girls, who quarreled over being allowed to be close to me.

I no longer know how long the games lasted that morning; neither do I know what we were thinking of, but instinctively we must have felt the impropriety, for we hid ourselves. While we spoke of all our other games at home, we kept silent about this one, as though we had agreed upon doing so.

I arrived at the dinner table late and sweaty that day, and it was not exactly pleasant to arrive late for a meal in the gray house.

After that, we often staged this game. I do not know what led us children to it and as much as I strain my memory, I can think of no incident that might explain these early sexual feelings in the other two, who were entirely normal children.

It was these games that first made me aware that there was a physical difference between the little girls and me. But as a child, of course, I was not entirely able to grasp the consequences of this discovery and was proud of what I considered to be a small advantage that my little girlfriends admired so much.

I have devoted so much space to this period, because I consider it interesting for two reasons, and not only significant as far as my natural disposition and inclinations are concerned. I have spoken of it mainly to draw the attention of parents and teachers to how early sexual feelings may arise in some children.

It was probably around this time when the first of several quarrels arose between my parents about my further education. Naturally, they did not carry on this battle in my presence. Even if they had, I would not have understood it or grasped its importance in terms of my entire life.

Somewhere in my memory, I do have a dim picture of an afternoon when two people are bent over my small bed, speaking to one another heatedly.

I do not know from which period this memory comes, nor whether it is connected with that quarrel between my parents, although the assumption is certainly justified.

My mother felt that my body was growing ever more masculine and that my character, too, showed more boy-like traits than those that are typical of girls. I was a healthy child who liked best to play noisy games with boys. All this made my mother worry, and she reminded her husband of his promise to consult a competent medical specialist.

My father shied away from the embarrassing fuss. He ridiculed Mother's worries, calling them exaggerated, and jokingly said that the worst thing that might happen would be that the child would be unable to marry, "and, you will admit that that is not the worst thing that can happen to a person." Probably my mother agreed, and with that, the whole matter was over and done with for a long time to come, as far as he was concerned.

My fifth birthday.

A short time earlier, we had welcomed a visitor who kindled our childish imagination. My godmother, a cousin of my father's, had come to Germany from Australia for a few months to see her family again. We found her a very interesting person, and she had risen in our esteem because of the lovely presents she had brought with her. And thus when my birthday approached, this time I was particularly looking forward to it.

I was woken up at eight o'clock. A little table that had been laid for me stood in my godmother's room. She was especially fond of children. Five candles were burning on the cake, and, blinking, I walked toward it.

There lay a doll, as big as I was. So that was the wonderful thing my godmother had promised me? *That* was what I had been so looking forward to? I could have cried, but just in time my eyes fell on a hobbyhorse, which my godmother, who had guessed my preferences, had added to the presents. To my mother, who disapproved, she apologized, saying that it had been added for the sake of completeness. Only then was I truly happy. Without saying thank you, and entirely ignoring the doll, I galloped away on my proud steed and, contemptuously, left everything else lying there. So even then I had no interest in girls' toys and a distinct inclination toward games for boys.

For lunch we had my favorite meal, as we always did on my birthday. While I devoted myself to the delights of rice pudding with raspberry sauce, paying full attention to the two delicacies, my father completed my bliss by giving me permission to work as I wished on a small plot in our garden from then on. I had been wanting that for a long time because Hilde had a small plot of her own, too. But she was stupid and did nothing sensible with it. I was sure that I would be wiser.

The next day, I immediately began gardening. I dug and shoveled, hoed and cleared the earth, and finally was faced with the great question of what I should plant. I was torn between radishes and flowers, and trotted back and forth along the adjoining garden paths, brooding. The gate rattled, and in came Hilde, carrying a little basket of flowers. "Look here, Nora, Mama cut these flowers for me. Let's plant them on your plot." She eagerly dug holes in the earth and firmly pressed the stems in. I watched her for a while, and then I lost my patience. "Take your flowers away. They won't grow!" I shouted, quite angrily, and tore the poor things out again. I felt so far above her girlish foolishness and so completely superior to her that unconsciously, I must have felt like a boy toward girl. For the time being, I preferred to plant weeds on my plot, for they grew roots and spread rampantly.

Working in the garden was my favorite pastime in those days. For variety, we went riding—Hilde, Leo, and I. Leo and I had far and away the most beautiful horses, ones with real bridles fastened to real heads. Poor Hilde could go in for the noble sport of horse riding only secretly, for her mother thought hobbyhorses were not really suitable toys for a girl. She had to make do with a stick, which looked poor between our thoroughbreds. Still, we trotted along very cheerfully. It was a sweet genre painting, two maids on hobbyhorses.

I remember that sometimes after riding, a strange feeling came over me, and today I tend to think the strange feeling was a slight degree of premature sexual arousal.

In order to stimulate this feeling, we galloped around wildly on our sticks.

Parents and teachers should be wary of giving children ill-chosen toys that might produce such premature erotic feelings. Rocking horses are a similar case.

Soon a great event took place in my life: the first day of school. I cannot really say that I was looking forward to it, because my siblings—especially my brother, who was a gifted but indolent student—had told me so many unpleasant things about school that I was inclined to see all teachers as nothing but masters of the rod. Occasional small hints in the streets, such as, "Look, Rascal, there goes your future lord and master," never failed to have an effect, and I began to hate teachers before I had ever seen the inside of a classroom. Children always feel with all their souls, both affection and hate; I forgot that I really only disliked my school tyrants, and transferred this feeling of dislike with unmotivated thoroughness to all the teachers in our town.

"Rascal," by the way, was the more descriptive than melodious name that my siblings had bestowed on me. At first, it was meant only as a joke, but after I had flown into a grotesque rage several times over it, the name stuck.

My parents tried to talk me out of my loathing for school but were not entirely successful. One day, Papa took me by the hand, and we went to the bookshop to buy me a slate and a primer.

It was the first time that I had been inside a bookshop, and a pleasant shiver ran down my spine when I saw all the books. Papa bought me a slate with a sponge and a stylus, and after purchasing the primer, we left well satisfied. Incidentally, the primer was a strange book; right on the first page was a picture of an ass. Mama taught me the black letters that stood under it. I eagerly traced them and soon acquired a certain skill. It caused me an odd pleasure to write the new word, "ass," on small scraps of paper and slip them to people in cases where I knew I could do so without fear of punishment.

The unpleasant feeling of duress that the word "school" had produced in me thus far receded slightly before the pleasant prospect of learning to read. My brother, Hans, sometimes read to us from *Leather-Stocking* in the evening, and I was so enthusiastic about Cooper's tales that for at least a fortnight I was determined to run away and secretly become an Indian. I was very keen on this plan, but Hans cooled off my longing considerably, for when we were making plans about how we would arrange our lives over there, he summarily allocated the role of his squaw to me.

Naturally, I was exceedingly angry about that, and with my fingernails tried to remove quite a few parts of his face, which I disliked very much at that moment. This project was obviously unpleasant for him; he defended himself, and our craving to run away degenerated into a serious brawl.

My loathing for school was noticeably diminished, for I hoped to learn to read quickly, and thus no longer be dependent on the good will of my brother.

I believe that all parents would succeed in making the work of teachers easier if they did not present school to their children as an instrument of control, but rather attempt to explain its pleasant aspects to them.

Soon after Easter, our lessons began. Papa took me to school the first day himself. On the way, he bought a cone of candy and handed it over, together with me, at school. I was led into a large room where there were many other children who seemed to feel just as uneasy as I did. Our names were called out, and we were sent to our seats. A large man in a black coat stepped up to the teacher's desk, and our first lesson began. When I think it over today, I believe that our preceptor was not, after all, the great mind we took him for. He had just arrived, fresh from teachers' training college.

While the teacher asked us our names, I looked around the classroom. Everything I saw aroused my displeasure. I certainly would not be staying here for long, most certainly not. Would the teacher be *very* angry if I ran away? A little blond girl, whom I had never seen, was sitting next to me. The child saw the tears that defiance had forced to my eyes, and said in a delicate little voice, "Don't cry. Otherwise, I will

be even more afraid. Come, hold my hand instead I'm so frightened."
She gave me her hand, and I wrapped my fingers around her small
suntanned hand. The knowledge that I had to protect this little thing,
who seemed so tiny to me, gave me a certain confidence and drove
away my fear of the new situation.

Thus, my first day at school would likely have passed peacefully, if
the teacher had not made a grave mistake at the end. He handed us
our cones of candy, accompanied by an unctuous speech, in which he
described them as a symbol of the sweet knowledge that school would
provide for us on our journey through life. The speech was surely
good, and I am certain I would understand it today; but at that time,
it was entirely impossible for me to do so. We looked far more expec-
tantly at his hands, which were doling out the candy, than at the honey
pouring from his lips. Suddenly, I sensed disaster, and yes, he handed
me a very small, miserable cone. "That's not my cone at all! Give me
back my cone!" I howled, infuriated. Thus ended my first day at school,
and my suffering began. For three days there was candy, and for three
days I liked school. On the fourth day, I discovered that nothing on
earth lasts forever, and on the sixth day my decision to run away was
made, and immediately executed. I asked the teacher whether I might
leave the room, and straight away, off I ran.

On the street, I ran into my father. I candidly confessed what had happened and was astonished when, without a moment's hesitation, he
took me back to school. That same day, I made another attempt to run
away, this time during the break, but some of the children held on to
me and called the teacher. He realized that ordinary methods would
not straighten me out, and so he bought me a sugarplum for two pfennigs. Thus peace was made once more.

Golden freedom was over. Most of my playmates, including those who
were my age, did not yet attend school; I was the first child from our
circle. At first, this privilege pleased me. But when I then had to learn
to write, I would gladly have given away all my dignity to spare myself

the agonizing procedure. I was entirely unable to grasp how one shaped individual lines into letters and was also long unable to learn the proper way to hold a pen, something on which our teacher placed a great deal of importance. I made a heroic decision. Three fingers are important; one holds the pen with them. And the forefinger appeared to play a particularly important role. With a burst of heroic strength, in an unguarded moment, I sawed away on that poor finger.

I no longer remember whether it was very painful. But the cut must have been fairly deep, because the scar is visible to this day. The only thing was that I made the mistake of cutting into my *left* finger, which was quite natural, for I wielded the knife in my right hand.

Finally, I learned how to write. I got on more easily in all the other subjects. I do not remember much about the nature of our lessons. I only recall one scene, which made me very jealous. Erna, my blond neighbor from the first day, continued to sit beside me. Our teacher had a habit of often kissing the little girls who were entrusted to him. He also handed out slices of apple during lessons, and if a girl had paid particular attention, she had to give him a kiss, and in return, received a piece of fruit. Erna was a very beautiful child, and most likely it was for this reason that she had the special privilege of being allowed to take the slice of apple from his mouth with her lips. I was jealous of Herr Meier because of this. We abhorred his lips and his big red hands. I seldom met with his marks of favor, which produced a strange conflict within me; I felt at once neglected and nauseated. To my knowledge, boys are never rewarded in this manner.

As difficult as writing was for me, I found reading all the easier. I quickly acquired a degree of skill. At the request of my mother, I was excused from needlework for the time being. My relationship with my siblings grew closer. I was no longer the whirlwind, able to enjoy unbridled freedom. Instead, like them, I had compulsory tasks, which we mostly did together in the evenings. For a time, school, with its discipline, had a soothing effect on me. I enjoyed the quiet work and sometimes was even permitted to join my sisters' games.

At that time, we had a maidservant of whom I was especially fond. Marie could tell wonderful stories of her country home and had won my heart one day by bringing me a rabbit. I was overjoyed but was not permitted to keep the animal. I had already made plans on how to feed it and had decided to sow grass all over my entire garden plot in place of the colorful flowers that I loved more than anything. Unfortunately, my joy soon ended, and my friendship with the servant was also marred. When Marie was bathing me one day, she whispered so much with the housemaid who had come into the room that I grew angry. They laughed long and loudly and left me sitting in the water, saying all manner of things about me, which I did not understand, but which were obviously nothing good. This irritated me no end, and my friendship with Marie quickly grew cold.

Until today, I know not how my mother divulged my secret to the servants and swore them to secrecy. For the maid who cared for me daily at least had to know of the matter.

The long winter evenings then became quite cozy. When we had finished our lessons, we sat down around the big games table. Hans read aloud; our two sisters sewed dolls' clothes, and I built colorful houses of cards or drew on a slate.

I recall the atmosphere on one evening during those years. It was after the evening meal. We were busily cutting out figures of ladies in an illustrated catalog from a firm in Berlin. We intended to play with the figures afterward. We were so absorbed that we did not say a word. One could hear only the tinkle of the scissors and the ponderous ticking of the old clock on the wall. From time to time, the fireplace crackled when a log was caught up by the greedy flames, or the fire leaped higher and for a moment threw flickering red light onto the pictures and mirrors. The reflection of the flames was also mirrored in warm tones on the surface of the oak furniture, which was brown with age.

We were used to keeping ourselves occupied, and had to make our own toys. An uncle had given Hans a fretsaw, which stood us in good stead and which was given to me when my brother grew older. It was a real treasure for me. Although my parents gave me a doll with dishes or similar girls' toys from time to time, those gave me no pleasure. I wanted proper boys' toys, especially as I grew older, but these wishes were denied to me for economic or other reasons, one of which was to keep me away from boyish things.

So the fretsaw was my greatest comfort. From the thin wood of old cigar boxes, I sawed out horses and wagons, cows and barnyard fowls—in short, everything that belongs on a farm—and then colored my little Noah's ark. I had only two colors at my disposal: a red pencil, which I had found in the wood yard; and a piece of chalk of unknown origin. Perhaps the animals were not very handsome; that did not matter, however, as I could play with them very well. And the hours I spent making the toys were often more pleasant than the games themselves.

I said earlier that our parents gave us few toys. I considered that a hardship in those days. Now, in the mature knowledge that my years of suffering have given me, I see clearly: anyone who wishes to save money by giving his children few toys is committing a criminal folly. Suitable playthings are like capital that one invests in the receptive souls of children, so that it may bear fruit. No child requires expensive toys; on the contrary, I am inclined to consider the rougher versions better, especially for younger children, than finely made, complicated playthings, because a child in his early years is able to take in simple lines and clear markings but unable to appreciate finer decoration. But it is even more important to give children with reasonable abilities unfinished materials and instructions on how to make toys out of them on their own. The joy of creating things is awakened, along with the child's joy of using the powers that lie within him. The child is encouraged to look, observe, and be creative, and where artistic talents are present, a healthy sphere for the imagination is opened up.

Observing little ones making toys is extremely interesting for those involved in research on children, and it teaches them to understand children's minds.

In many cases, I have observed that there is usually a clear difference between the games the two sexes play. There was a pile of clay in a neighbor's yard. Our crowd of children often played there. It was easy to mold the clay. While the girls attempted to knead pots from the soft material, or make naively and grotesquely shaped stoves for their dolls, the boys rolled balls and formed the clay into animals. Like the boys, I made myself balls for my slingshot or tried to form human figures or animals. A child who wants to saw a cow out of wood or mold it from clay must first look closely at the living animal. In addition to the child's developing a sense of form, his powers of observation are made keener, and he gains a closer relationship to nature. Every creative child is, in a sense, an artist, a future human being who, in his individual development, illustrates the development of the entire human race. It may safely be said that a child who lovingly and keenly wishes to reproduce the body of an animal will try to protect the living model—and likewise, all other living creatures—from torment. The drive to destroy things, which is inherent in every person and which is most alive in children who have not yet learned the falsehood of being moderate, will be diminished to a reasonable measure by creative efforts.

Gradually, I learned that school and attending school had their pleasant sides, after all. Until now, Hans had exercised intolerable tyranny over me. When I asked him to read to me, it always cost me my best things—for example, the first radishes from my garden plot or anything else that happened to elicit his greed. Now I was in a better position, for I could read those books about Indians, which I then considered so splendid, myself. Glowing with enthusiasm, I read my way through the whole pile. I soon was gripped by a reading fever. At the age of nine, I was already reading novels published in the magazine *Die Gartenlaube*, stories by Marlitt and such things. This did me no harm. The books about Indians made the deepest impression on me. The description of the free and unrestrained life and the heroic deeds of the noble redskins greatly attracted me, and Chingachcook, the Great Snake, was the only man for whom I ever had enraptured feelings.

Today I think differently about the worth of those books about Indians. I think we are doing the life of our nation a disservice by placing those books in our sons' hands. Especially during the years when enthusiasm is easily kindled, we should give them *German* books. In legend and history, we have many a great man whose deeds they might relish and enthuse over. At that time, those Indian heroes delighted me and made me so enthusiastic that I never stopped thinking about them.

When I was not sitting in the garden, bent over a thick book, I was playing with my two little friends. Hilde, Lene, and I still faithfully played together. We had forgotten the aforementioned games at last, no doubt, and devoted ourselves to more harmless pleasures.

It was spring again, and the game of the season was rolling marbles. It was great fun because we crouched on the ground and soiled our hands and clothing. Mama did not like to see me joining in this game. I thought she considered the game too dirty, whereas she actually had other reasons, which I was to comprehend only later.

One early evening in spring, we were playing marbles on the road. Our place was well chosen because there are any number of holes in the paved roads of Bergheim, and the grass was not yet tall enough to keep our marbles from rolling. I had just played a good game and won three fat glass marbles from Lene when I looked up and noticed how both Lene and Hilde were staring at me, giggling and whispering. They pointed to my dress, which had flown up in the heat of the game. Shocked and ashamed, I stood up. We did not continue with our game that day. I soon forgot the incident; however, after that, I paid more attention to my dress when playing, and to the others' dresses, too.

I had just begun my ninth year when I left the preparatory classes and joined the girls' lyceum. I found this natural and proper for a child of my social class. I believe that at that time, I had entirely lost my awareness of the physical difference between myself and other little girls, or did not understand the meaning of it.

I had not been in the youngest class at the girls' school for more than six months, and had hardly begun to feel at home in a new circle when, for the first time, I became conscious of the heavy burden of suffering that a hard fate had placed upon me.

Until now, I had been excused from needlework at the request of my mother; now I had to participate, as it was obligatory at this school. When knitting, my awkward fingers could not hold the needles, and my sewing was the worst in the whole class, and the most untidy, too, because it kept having to be unpicked. No piece of work could be done without reprimands or severe punishment. "You really are as clumsy as a boy," the teacher often scolded me. That made me hate all the subjects taught by female teachers, whereas I found the scientific subjects taught by male teachers interesting—until an incident ruined the entire school for me.

Until then, I had been popular among my schoolmates, so it surprised me all the more when I noticed that for some time, the children had been withdrawing from me and playing without me. I did not understand this until, one day, the terrible blow came. I have only a dark memory. All the tears I shed then lie between me and those times, much suffering and many a dark hour.

I shall attempt to tell you what happened then. It was during a recess period. Rain had kept us in the classrooms. The girls were playing some kind of singing game; I still feel as though I can hear the lost sound of a rhyme in my ear. I quickly shut my books and ran to join the game, but none of the girls would speak to me or let me into their circle. Timidly, I asked why, but no one answered me. Hilde looked aside in embarrassment, and at last Lene burst out, "Go away, you nasty boy, you, we don't want to play with boys!" I did not understand her at all. "You're a proper boy, we know that for sure, and Fräulein Stieler says so, too, and that's why you can't knit. Go away and play with boys!"

That hurt. I did not know where the girls had gotten their knowledge.

Had Hilde and Lene talked about those old forgotten games, or of the afternoon when we crouched, playing in the street?

All this crossed my mind in a flash, and I felt darkly that it would be a great misfortune for me if I were unable to make the girls change their minds.

I did not know what to say, as much as I brooded. But I raged and shouted and tried to convince the girls that I surely was a girl, too. I was just about to undo my skirts when the teacher entered the room. That was the end of the quarrel for that day but not of the burden that now weighed on me. In the evening, when I was alone in my room, I looked at my body. It was simply not true! I was not a boy! Mama called me her little girl, and she had tears in her eyes, and when mothers have tears in their eyes, they most certainly are speaking the whole truth, I knew that. No, I certainly was a girl; that is why I was so often sad about tearing my clothing when I climbed trees. But in spite of all these arguments, I could not fall asleep that night, but lay wide awake for a long time, pondering things. Being brought up as a girl, being called by a girl's name had had a suggestive influence on me. I had long forgotten the old games or placed no importance on those differences, and was entirely convinced that I was a girl, just a bit different from most, which did not appear at all strange to me. Since my nature was different from all theirs, why should my body not be so, too? I was almost reassured again. And then, all at once I became conscious: yes, the others, down there, they were certainly very different! And a nameless fright took hold of me. I decided to appeal to my mother first thing in the morning.

When morning came, I meant to ask the fatal question. But I was afraid of my mother's wide eyes, in which I thought I would read reproach, so what I had wanted to ask her remained unsaid. On the way to school, I trembled with fright, and in despair, I entered. Right away, I was greeted with the same shouts as the day before, and was even sadder. The beginning of lessons always brought me salvation; the recess periods meant torment once again.

And thus a year full of terrible problems came to an end. I was so very afraid of school. At home, I sat in my corner in distress, brooding. Yes, I surely was a boy, I was certain of this now. But why had they given me a girl's name? Why was my brother, Hans, allowed to enjoy life and not me? I pondered and pondered, and was unable to get to the bottom of the riddle. Then, by chance, I read the story of Achilles, whose mother gave him female garments. With feverish excitement, I read the legend to the end. I rejoiced. I was saved! And a sudden awakening of arrogance shielded me from the taunts of my comrades. Yes, that was how it was and how it had to be: I was a prince who was being raised far from his parents. I was only still undecided whether I was a stolen prince, or whether my royal parents had sent me to distant places on purpose, in order that worthy burghers might raise me.

Thus, at the age of ten, I had lost all sense of reality. The girls pushed me aside, and I retreated into myself. I usually crouched in a corner with a book. From somewhere I had gotten an interesting book: *Legends of Antiquity*. This gave new food to my dreams. It was written there: Achilles grew up in girls' clothing, and Oedipus was sent by his parents into the mountains, that was the same thing.

Thus I found a new lease on life, depending on my books and doing without children's games, in a world of my own. The torture of having to sit next to my tormentors during lessons was the only thing that kept me in the real world.

I am thinking of summer evenings. Our parents would sit in front of the door leading to the wood yard. The voices of my siblings echoed from the playground. The evening wind carried the aroma of resin from the freshly cut fir trees. In silent, ghostly haste, bats snapped for their prey. I was sitting with my parents on the bench, when the splashing of the fountain, which lay in the twilight of the summer evening, drifted by my ear. Surely, I was the son of a king. The ordinary old fountain had become a glorious well of healing. I drank the first sip and presented the water to my faithful burghers of Bergheim. The tinkling of the glass breaking on the flagstones wakes me up and, unfortunately, my mother as well.

The fountain is often in my thoughts. Once, when I was punished for a bad habit, I dreamed of the time when I would, at last, be king. I would stop up the water pipes and let all the citizens of Bergheim die of thirst. Naturally, a prince cannot go on foot, and so I rode daily through the town on Arabian steeds. These Arabians were wild and reared up. I was often hard pressed to subdue the wild animals. The adults, with their tired, foolish eyes, did not see this and shook their heads when they saw me leaping along. Aunt Liese often scolded me or knocked on the window when I passed her house, and often said to my mother how nice it would be if I would only, at least once, walk along decorously, like other little girls. But all in all, I did not go out into the streets much. I mostly sat quietly in the garden with a book or played with toys that I had made myself. My parents wondered what had suddenly turned the once much-too-wild girl into an earnest stay-at-home. But tell them what the girls had said to me? I would not have been able to do so. Inside, we were all strangers to one another. My mother carried many a heavy burden; Father, with the egoism of all invalids, thought only of himself.

The brooding earnestness and unnatural quiet could not always prevail in the face of my wildness, and I suffered from my loneliness. The girls had made me thoroughly hate them. I tried approaching the boys, but that was very difficult. In the end, I did sometimes play with Hans and Leo, the sons of a merchant with whom Papa was friendly. It was not at all easy to be taken seriously by the boys. At first, they always looked at me scornfully so I racked my brains for a heroic deed that would prove my courage to them. They had said that girls were sissies; that was why no real boy should play with a girl. But I was no sissy and wanted to prove it to them. One day when we were together, I took a sheet of paper, crumpled it into a ball, and set it on fire. I held it in my hand until it burned out, but I did not cry out, although I was trembling with pain. My entire hand was burned. I then challenged the boys to follow my example, but neither of the two had the courage to do so. They both backed off from this fiery test. With my courage, I had finally won their trust. I was happy and would have burned my other hand as well, but Hans, the older of the two, would not allow it. Soon, other boys joined our games. The wildest of all the playmates was me. Often we went into the woods, where one of us would read Indian stories aloud and the others would sit in a circle around him. We lived through those stories from the books ourselves, and named ourselves after the characters we especially liked. I was Chingachcook. We sat before invisible fires, piles of twigs, which were, of course, not lit, and smoked equally invisible peace pipes, took off our boots and crept barefoot through the woods so as not to leave any traces for our "enemies," the Iroquois. Like Chingachcook and Unkas, the fleet-footed deer, we crawled on our bellies to the enemy camp, which was not always to the advantage of our clothing, and hardly pleased our parents. We had carved ourselves weapons from wood. Mysteriously, Wally, my oldest sister's doll, lost her wig made of genuine hair, and, just as mysteriously, a chopping knife that had graced my mother's kitchen for many years disappeared. These things and others reappeared in the woods hanging from my belt, and I was envied the "real" scalp and the shining tomahawk no end. Here, with the boys, I was in my element and, in spite of my girls' clothing, was considered an equal comrade with full rights.

Once, we had to swim across a wide river in pursuit of the Iroquois. The river, which was perhaps two meters in width and at least forty centimeters deep, was called by us the Saint Lawrence, and farther back there, where the red roofs shone, lay Montreal. The great Chingachcook took off his shoes and wanted to wade through the brook; next to him, of course, was young Unkas. Everything would have been well, but the unhappy Unkas lost his balance, and we both tumbled into the water. Soaking wet, we came ashore. We undressed and laid out our clothing to dry in the sun. None of the boys found anything untoward about me, and I was glad of that.

My parents would probably never have learned of the incident, if I had not, in the heat of the game, mixed up my hunting shirt with Unkas's. Thus, the maid was not a little surprised when she undressed me that evening.

That adventure, which had unpleasant consequences for me, and the pirate stories, which were being read a lot at that time, drew our attention to water games. We carved ourselves ships, which we floated in the old moat, and finally hit upon the idea of playing a ship's crew. That was certainly a fine idea! The ranks were distributed: there was a captain, a deck officer, sea cadets, two helmsmen, and a steward; in short, everyone was there, but I cannot remember whether we had any ordinary seamen. But our future lay not on the water, but in the wood yard. We had a sailboat there: the tall fir trees that good-natured workmen had stood upright for us were the masts upon which I often sent my crew to see whether a warship was coming; for *we* were pirates.

Yes, we were the crew of a pirate ship called the *Red Falcon,* which occasionally loaded slaves, too. Leo, our helmsman, was very cruel to the poor rabble. He broke the blackamoors' arms and legs; sometimes he even beheaded one. If he went too far, my mother thrashed me. She was willing to give us her blackamoors to play with, but not to have us destroy them. "What shall I cook, if you stamp everything to pieces?" For these blackamoors, who we claimed were wild Negroes, were harmless heads of cabbage.

Through a kind of coup d'état, I had risen to the rank of captain of the *Red Falcon.* I ruled my crew with strict discipline and was much feared by mutineers because of my dashing airs.

For the rest of the day, the freedom of these wild games made me forget how I suffered during lessons. But the next morning on my way to school, fear took hold of me once more.

By accident, I witnessed a scene from the life of animals, which gripped me and occupied my thoughts for a long time. Numerous swallows' nests were stuck to the low roofs of the old storehouses that surrounded our yard on four sides. I spent many an hour watching the graceful little birds. In summer, I liked to lie on the grass and watch the swallows crisscrossing through the air with their loud calls.

In winter, too, we found the nests interesting when cheeky sparrows occupied them and lived comfortably in strangers' homes. The best time was spring, when the swallows returned and searched for their old nests with joyful chirping. One day, my sister showed me a flock of swallows busily flying around a nest and chirping loudly. She told me that the swallows fought with the sparrows, and any little gray bird that would not leave his winter quarters voluntarily would be immured alive in the nest by the swallows.

An indescribable horror seized me, and for the first time I felt the tragedy of the struggle for survival tremble within me. Since that day, I have hated swallows and felt a comradely affection for those cheeky street urchins, the sparrows. I found a certain similarity in our fates: they were chased away by the swallows, and I was pushed out of their circle by the girls. I often mulled this over.

Of all the fairy tales I read, I liked the one about the Ugly Duckling best of all. I felt as though Andersen's fairy tale had a secret relationship to me. I cherished a constant hope for some kind of happiness, which life still owed me.

At that time, an amusing episode took place, which unfortunately ended in tragedy. We had seen that my brother smoked. It seemed wonderful to me to be able to swallow fire, and since we still played many Indian games it was really essential, in the interest of a realistic performance, to pass the peace pipe from mouth to mouth. Enviously, we looked up to Hans and his friends, who had founded a smokers' club. This notable club gave our parents little pleasure. They were unable to explain to themselves their son's pale and distraught appearance, which returned at regular intervals, especially toward evening.

We were envious, but it was difficult to know what to do, as the cigarettes we longed for were expensive. We tried smoking with pieces of cane taken from a broken carpet beater, which we set alight, and from which we actually got smoke into our mouths when we drew on them.

We tried out our new invention one afternoon in our dining room when mother was out walking and father was in the office. When Mama returned, she asked Sofie, the maid, whether she had been burning rags or hair, of all things. The maid protested at this accusation but did not betray us. However, she gave us the good advice to wallow in our pleasures outdoors in the future.

That evening, I could hardly eat, and my parents wondered whether, in the end, an epidemic disease was not holding sway in Bergheim. The next day we moved outdoors. The sticks in our mouths, croaking and writhing in inner torture, we wandered between tall hedges, which hid us from unwanted eyes. But it was by no means a joyous march. From time to time, one or another of us fell back, overcome by an irresistible desire for solitude. At a crossing of paths, we collided with a man who laughed londly at the sight of our dismal faces. It was "Uncle Richard," not my real uncle, but the uncle of all the children in Bergheim.

He explained to us that this was not true smoking; for that, one needed a pipe. And straightaway, he gave us his old pipe, which he happened to have with him. He also suggested a good mixture of tobacco. "You have to dry potato foliage and mix it half and half with chestnut leaves, and then you'll have an excellent kind of tobacco," he advised us.

A few days later, the tobacco was ready. My comrades had bought themselves pipes, I had proudly armed myself with Uncle Richard's old one. We climbed up into an old attic and looked for the remotest corner, as we felt most secure there. After we had pulled up the ladder for added security, we began puffing away. The smoke rose through the low, rotting ceiling and drifted merrily into the clear summer air.

We had not devoted ourselves to the pleasure for long when we suddenly felt terribly ill, most awfully ill, actually. But none of us would have thrown away his pipe, heaven forbid! We stared ahead and smoked. An inexplicable, dreamy heaviness weighed on us, from which we were suddenly jolted awake.

What was that? Was someone not shouting "fire!"? It seemed to be Papa's voice. We rushed to the trapdoor, climbed down the hastily fetched ladder and stood face-to-face with our workers. For when Papa had seen the puffs of smoke rising above the roof of the old shed, he had thought that the stock of wood had caught fire, and had called the workers together. His mood did not exactly improve when he saw that we were the cause of his fright, and the reception he gave us was decidedly unpleasant. As a result of this adventure, I was forbidden to associate with boys from then on. But secretly, I spent much time with them, as I now felt that I belonged with them.

Gradually, the girls seemed to have forgotten the event that had been so hurtful to me, and only occasionally one or another of them would shout an ugly word. Incidentally, the street urchins also shouted "Norbert" after me. All the children knew that there was something odd about me. Whether the adults knew it, too, I cannot say. Unfortunately, my parents persisted in their silence. One single clarifying word would surely have sufficed to set me free, and I cannot comprehend that they left that word unsaid! In my view, my parents should have made a particular effort to approach me in a friendly way. But I was left on my own.

Perhaps my parents did not know how widespread the knowledge of my oddness was among the children. There is a kind of freemasonry among children; a word can be known by everyone for a long time in the land of children before the grown ups hear it. Especially the things they secretly tell one another of sexual matters: these are understandably never mentioned before adults.

The girls sometimes allowed me to play with them now. Our greatest pleasure was playing school. It was summer, and once again we played under the old eldertree arbor. We all sat on the bench or crouched in the sand. Only one of the girls, who pretended to be the teacher, stood with a thin little stick in the middle of the space. The teacher asked questions, we deliberately gave wrong answers, and then the teacher called the stupid pupil to her side and went with her into a corner, where she lifted the pupil's dress and beat her. I enjoyed playing teacher in this game but was terribly afraid of exposing myself to the eyes of the others. For that reason, I always gave the correct answer, although that did not really count, for the main pleasure lay not in playing school, but rather in the beating. I always trembled with fear that I would be found out as a boy and sent away.

It is clear that under those circumstances, I did not feel particularly at ease among the girls. I repeatedly attempted to lure the girls away from this game and to interest them in my wild boys' games. Sometimes I succeeded. We played wild running games until the teachers forbade them. My influence or rather, my example had an unruly effect on the others. When Erna, my friend from the house next door, and I visited one another, we never used the gate that connected our parents' properties, but rather climbed over the dividing wall.

Now and again a fantastical streak, which sprang from my dreams, ran through our games. I had read a story about a boy whose father was an Indian of noble birth. The lad was raised in Germany, and as a youth returned to the country of his birth to claim his inheritance from his father. There he tamed a tigress. This made a deep impression on me, I thought that the skin of the tiger, which was always pictured standing next to its master in the brilliantly colored pictures in the book, was just like a traveling rug with which Papa was in the habit of covering himself during his afternoon nap. I loved to spread the rug out before me and dream of how I would tame the tiger. I hid these dreams from all the adults and did not speak of them to my playmates, either, occasionally, these colorful dream images shimmered in our games, which I usually led.

Soon I had become so wholeheartedly involved in these games that I found a cage for the animal in one of the attics. Lotti Krumane was an especially close friend at that time, a little blond girl with a rather foolish expression. I showed her my treasure and the cage, too, which was an abandoned hen coop. She helped me look for food, because such a wild animal does eat a large amount.

Well, there was plenty of food: the bloodthirsty animal got compressed hay, which we stole from the stable. I greatly impressed my little play-mate by the courage I displayed in calmly sticking my hand into the cage of this "wild beast."

We felt pleasantly frightened when we climbed the small ladder, afraid at every step that the "tiger" might attack us.

Although I was extremely clumsy at needlework in school, I was re-markably gifted and very interested in crafts. I could spend hours sit-ting next to our cobbler, watching him, as he mended a pair of boots.

I had connected Erna's window to mine with wire, so that we could send each other "important" messages. We did this with the help of two small empty tin boxes, which we pulled back and forth on strings. Although we saw each other about ten times a day, it was still very exciting to be connected by such a private postal service, which we proudly called our telephone. We enjoyed this for a long time, until one day Leo had the bright idea to tie the feet of a frog together and place it in the little box from which Erna took her letters. We hid and soon saw Erna pull the box toward her, visibly pleased by its unusual heaviness. Just as she was about to look in, a big frog jumped out at her. The prank was all the more nasty because we knew that Erna was terrified of frogs.

I was bolder and more boyish; I once collected 136 of those small gray land frogs, which liven up the puddles in summer after every rain. I kept this treasure in a cigar box, under fresh leaves, and was only sur-passed by Leo, who one day increased his menagerie to all of 159. Erna had once called our treasure "disgusting old frogs," and to get even with her for that, we had sacrificed the largest specimen in our collection.

I mention the frog episode here, which in itself is quite trivial, be-cause it seems to be noteworthy when assessing my natural disposition.

This instinctive manner of playing was so unusual in a girl that my parents would surely have discerned my sex if they had only wanted to, even disregarding my physique. But they simply did not want to see!

Setting traps, an activity in which I engaged enthusiastically, was also very unfeminine. I hardly think a real girl would climb up a tree to catch a bird or set up traps the way I did.

I was usually the mastermind behind my playmates' boyish pranks, although, as a pupil at a girls' school, I was not permitted to take part in the execution of the plans.

Shortly before my twelfth birthday, a mighty fear entered my life. In the middle of summer, without having had a cold beforehand, I became hoarse.

My voice lost its timbre and had no strength, it changed from the highest of trebles to the deepest of basses. Others found this amusing, but I was very disconcerted.

By coincidence, I read in a book that consumptives are often hoarse. Now I knew what was wrong with me, and in my lively imagination I thought I felt all the symptoms mentioned in the book. I coughed, suffered from backaches, and even our wild games, of which I was so fond, caused me problems. It was definitely consumption, and I felt that surely I must die. These thoughts clouded my childish joie de vivre. Soon I would have to die and leave our gray house, the dear wood yard, the tranquil sunny streets of my town, and everything I loved.

Even today, I can still feel trembling within me, the melancholy that then engulfed my entire life, the sadness that completely dominated my existence. The gray house seemed kind and friendly when I considered how soon I was to leave it. I thought long and hard about my life, and when for some reason the thought took hold of me that the end must surely come before autumn, I went walking through our house and into the yard, sadly taking leave. Languidly, I stroked the old walls of the house, which all at once seemed kind and familiar. During the long summer evenings when all were resting, I liked best to sit in the yard in solitude. In the fading daylight, the objects no longer cast shadows, the outlines became unclear and blurred, and only where the moonlight fell was it brighter and the shadows deeper.

The dry leaves rustled softly in the breeze, and when a stronger wind arose, the narrow boards, which stood upright, knocked gently against one another. Here and there, through the garden fence, a rose shone like a red star; ivy hung over the metal rods, black as night. The last birds wearily sought their nests; only bats came forth from the old roofs, circling darkly in the sky.

There I liked to sit on the ground in a corner of the yard, my head lost in thought, leaning against a tree. Over the shadow-bordered world of the yard lay a vastness, which gently delivered me from my insignificant, arrogant child's dream of being a prince.

It was perfectly still. Only the croaking of a frog echoed now and then through the air. The fountain splashed dreamily in the quiet songs of the night. We are one, gushed the fountain, rattled the boards shaken by the wind, and murmured the dry leaves. In this lonely sorrow, my thoughts of death became ever stronger and more certain, and when I lay in my bed, I cried for a long while, full of scalding self-pity.

For days, I went into the woods and greeted the places that had witnessed our happy Indian games. I walked across the yard and through the house and thought about leaving my home. A mildness, otherwise quite foreign to me, lay over my nature. I was fond of everyone and forgave my parents the injustice of raising the boy I felt myself to be as a girl. I forgave my little tormentors at school all their brutality and the teasing with which they had so often tortured me.

I liked going to the churchyard, and chose myself a plot. I wanted to lie near the wall where two tall hawthorn bushes rain down blossoms every spring.

Everyone noticed my changed voice, but no one told me that it was not an illness but the breaking of my voice that had changed it.

When the condition had gone on for weeks and the first leaves on the trees began to turn russet as a sign of the approaching autumn, I began, in my fear, to prepare myself for death.

Religious instruction, which was taught in the upper classes of the girls' school by an old clergyman, made an especially strong impression on me. The clergyman was able to understand my searching soul. For him, there was no light in the world and no joy. He showed us a gloomy, bleak world. For him, God was not a loving, but rather an angry, father. I understood this well. I felt, as he did, how many sins lay on the world, on each individual, and on me. And I felt the sins that lay on me growing immeasurably: What was to become of the world in all this misery? Would all be ruined? Could no one redeem it?

Then I recalled the fear that we children felt when awaiting collective punishment. We mostly drew lots then, and the one who drew the shortest straw had to take upon himself the guilt and punishment for all.

I assumed that this childish custom would also apply to the good Lord. Perhaps he would forgive the rest of the world if one person took on all the guilt and punishment and expressed penitence through remorse and death. The mystical words "Son of Man" appealed to me. Suddenly, my task stood clearly before my eyes. I, a poor lonely child, had been chosen to take all the suffering of the world upon myself so that the world would be delivered of all suffering. I grew more and more accustomed to the thought. I imagined that I could feel the power of my soul growing and thought that I was receiving immeasurable wisdom. I read the Bible with ecstatic fervor, until the weighty rhythm of its verses intoxicated me. I thought then that I knew everything. To fulfill the words of the prophets, I, God's sacrifice dressed in the robes of the poor, had to live in the poorest of all robes, in "women's skirts," so as to taste all the vileness of the world. I understood why Jesus had not yet fully redeemed the world. Yes, he had suffered much, he had become human, but he had lived as a *man*, and had not gone through the abasement of life as a woman as well.

The more I sank into such brooding, the clearer these ideas became. I thought that I heard voices and spoke with angels who surrounded

me. In a dreamy ecstasy one night, I heard God say to me in a kindly
voice, "dear son."

All my childish actions from then on were connected with religious
thoughts. I constantly felt close to God.

I had expected death to come with autumn. But when autumn passed
and winter, too, drew to a close without my dying, these ideas started
to fade. When spring arrived, it brought back my former joie de vivre,
and I took great pleasure in having been returned to life. When I saw
that nothing more threatened me, when Hans and Leo also became
hoarse and proudly declared, "Our voices are breaking. That's what
happens to all boys!" the last shred of my worry disappeared. So, too,
did my celestial thoughts.

Those images faded gradually altogether but, left over from those
days, I still feel a deep reverence for everything connected with reli-
gion and faith.

Soon afterward, I had a discussion with my little friends that caused
our friendship to suffer a severe breach, without my being able today
to say what the reason for that may have been.

It was a splendid spring day that, with its shining beauty, filled one's
breast with joy. We were strolling across the wood yard looking for
adventure when we suddenly stood before the "wreck" of the *Red Falcon*.
A few ropes, which the woodyard hands had not yet retrieved, were
swinging back and forth in the March wind. We climbed up high for
practice, hung comfortably from the rigging, and began to chat.
Abruptly, Hans asked me, "Say, Rascal, would you like to be a proper
boy?" And he went to great lengths to make it clear how proper I should
become in his view.

Now I do not know what my thoughts were then, but I was extremely
annoyed with my comrades, who in their boasting thought they were
so grand, and I began to brag about how good girls had it, and how
pleased I was to be a girl, too. At that moment, my eyes were filled

with tears, likely tears of joy. Hans and Leo listened to me, smiling scornfully, and laughing loudly, bade me farewell. "Adieu, dear Nora, sweet little thing, go and play nicely with your dolls." "Old squaw!" Leo called back to me from the garden gate.

That was too much for me to bear. I slithered quickly down my rope and gave him a sound thrashing. That was the last time we played together.

The school was putting on a patriotic play, in which all pupils were participating; only I had been left out. I felt hurt by this, and on Papa's advice I screwed up my courage and asked a teacher why I had been excluded. The lady smiled in embarrassment and said, "Well, you see, dear child, we are doing it in your own interest, for it cannot possibly be pleasant for you if so many people hear your voice."

Sadly, I went home and told Papa what the teacher had said to me. He shrugged his shoulders and said something about the bigotry of all teachers, and of those who lived in Bergheim in particular, and then appeared to be satisfied. He left me alone with my tormented thoughts.

Being pushed aside did nothing to spur me to work hard. I always did my homework at the last possible hour, and I was all the more able to do so as I found it quite easy. I was neither diligent nor ambitious; there would have been no point. I could not have gained a higher position in school, no matter how hard I might have worked. We had a fixed ranking, as uncompromising as a court ceremonial. The highest position in the class was occupied by the headmaster's daughter; the second "belonged" to the niece of the duke's house marshal; and the third to the dear daughter of our mayor. The fourth place, which was the highest that one could attain, was mine.

None of us liked the teachers. They were two old spinsters, one of them bitter, caustic, and astute, but only keen to torment us pupils with her wisdom; the other was narrow-minded. Above all, both were too old to feel in touch with youth. They took every word as a personal insult. We despised our teachers or, at best, feared them. I thought then that the relationship between teachers and pupils was always disagreeable, so I was very surprised when, in later years, I became acquainted with the friendly understanding that so often binds pupils and teachers.

The school play I mentioned gave us food for conversation long afterward. It awakened a real passion for the theater, which especially took hold of my class. We were always playing theater, and did so with great enthusiasm. Naturally, we had neither props nor costumes, but we did not miss such trivial details. The male parts fell naturally to me, without my making an effort to get them. The girls instinctively felt the masculinity of my nature.

For weeks, we acted in every spare moment; we acted in the woods, in the garden, under the old elder-tree arbor and in our yard, until Uncle Richard kindly let us use his old storeroom. That was a splendid temple of the Muses. True, the barrels of petroleum and oil, which had once been stacked there, had left behind their odors, but that did not dampen our enthusiasm. We dramatized poems for our performances. One of them was Uhland's *The Good Fortune of Edenhall.* Scene: the storeroom. The Lord (that was me) is seated at the table with several maidens. Hilde was the cupbearer. At the words "hesitantly draws forth from the silken cloth the tall crystal chalice," she unwrapped a tiny schnapps glass from a red rag. Uncle Richard, who was our entire audience, beamed all over, probably with delight at our meticulous production.

"In storms the enemy, bringing fire and death"—with a sudden howl, Lene burst onto the stage from the auditorium, where she had been waiting until now, for we lacked a pit or a backdrop. At "by the sword the young Lord falls," the whole thing was so comical that I had to laugh in spite of my death. I behaved badly, and as payment for this extra performance, which was not envisaged in the program, I recieved a proper thrashing from my older and stronger partner.

I had had enough of art. My sturdy colleague had driven away my longing for the stage.

The boys were forbidden to enter our theater. Thus, we only saw each other from time to time in the street, and greeted each other or walked together for a few steps in the dusk.

Common interests connected with school bound me to the girls. Since I had discovered that the teachers did not notice when my sister Lotte did my needlework, this torture was no longer so terrible. For five pfennigs, Lotte was willing to sew the longest of seams by hand.

Meanwhile, I had become a person to be reckoned with in class. I wrote the best compositions, which the others took advantage of. Often I wrote three or four compositions for others before I began work on my own. Sometimes not many ideas were left for my own work. Occasionally, the teacher then held up the compositions by the top pupil, which *I* had written, to me as an example. Scarcely had I rid myself of the torture of needlework, when another subject that I hated almost as much became part of our curriculum.

In girls' schools, the older students were taught dancing in gym class. I found this unspeakably loathsome. I was shockingly ungraceful and knew as little about what to do with my limbs as other boys of my age. I hated "hopping about" from the bottom of my heart. On dancing days, I went to gym classes unwillingly, sometimes wishing that an earthquake, a broken leg, or some other unpleasantness might save me from this kind of gym. Gym class used to be my favorite, something to which I looked forward all week. I just could not work up any enthusiasm for dancing.

My favorite subject was natural history. I found anthropology most fascinating. I had now realized that I could not understand the secret that was wrapped around my strangeness by brooding over theories. Thus I waited with bated breath in natural history lessons for a word that might have guided me onto the right path. My main passion was for medicine. In the old attic, where the cage for my imaginary tiger still stood, I set up a laboratory. There I dissected mice and frogs. I intended to study medicine when I was older. Although I had never heard of women going to university, I was sure I could have my way. I did not waste a thought on how.

Things erotic were becoming of more and more interest at the girls' school. At first, I was nauseated by the manner in which they spoke of the delicate secrets that join the two sexes. But seeing as my fellow pupils listened with relish to the smutty revelations of those who knew the facts of life, I, too, became interested in these things. They laughed in scorn at the absurd fairy tale of the stork. Let the foolish believe that; we knew better where babies came from. A nursemaid introduced us in more detail to the subject in her own way.

In school, we had hotly debated whether all adults did "it," and in general had come to the conclusion that they did, but stoutly defended our own parents, who certainly had never done "a thing like that." On the way home, Hilde and I brooded over what we had heard and whispered eagerly, wondering whether everything was to be believed. We were bothered by all sorts of doubts, which we immediately entrusted to old Nine, who cared for Hilde's little sister. We received our first sexual revelations from this nursemaid. We listened, excited and breathless. Entirely new and hitherto unknown feelings flashed through us, and Hilde squeezed my hands as if she would break them.

How could anyone be so "foolish"? the nursemaid wondered. She told us that it was ancient knowledge and written in the Bible and that we should go ahead and look it up. Certainly, all adults did it, and the children arrived in thus a way. Childbirth was very painful. The women become fatter day by day until, well, we would soon see. "Just look at Hilde's mother," she ended her sermon. We looked at her. The nursemaid was right, and Hilde's childish faith was shaken. Her whole soul suffered; the great admiration she had always felt for her mother was diminished, and the childish belief in her, in a person who abandoned herself to such ugly sins, was shaken. For it must be sin and ugliness; why else would it have been kept hidden?

This story may be an isolated case, perhaps not. Why do mothers allow their sacred rights to be stolen from them? They would not suffer a servant in their homes who stole their old clothes or caps, but that the souls of their children are stolen and besmirched goes unnoticed.

Months had passed. We had digested the new knowledge. Eagerly, everything we imagined or actually experienced was related. When, during a walk, Hilde and I saw the love play of two dogs, we watched the event, breathless with suspense. It was on a lonely country road outside the town where no one saw how eagerly we watched the animals. An insane excitement took hold of us. Hilde threw herself onto the ground and laughed hysterically. I was afraid of her laughter, which I did not understand. I feared her eyes and her hands, which reached out for me. Although I wished to feel those hands on my body, the fear of betraying my secret to her once again overrode my feelings, and I withdrew from her caresses.

In school, a strange and sinister hustle and bustle prevailed. The girls were beginning to grow. The angles of their childish bodies began to soften into slender, maidenly curves. The secret sexual power that began to stir in them haunted their little brains day and night. Formerly, we had talked about our favorite games or the girls had discussed their dolls. But now all other interests vanished from our horizon, and the interest in things sexual and erotic dominated.

The girls opened their dresses and showed one another their breasts. "Look, I have a figure already!" It aroused the strongest envy when one of them was well endowed in that way. The youthful forms were touched, and some girls confided in us with secret pride, "I have hair under my arms, you know." No boy could boast more about his first facial hair than these girls did about their gifts from nature.

A dark matter now cast its shadow far ahead of me: menstruation.

Everyone wanted to be the first to experience this miracle. In some, this wish became so intense that it culminated in ardent prayers. Why did they long for it?

Partly so as to be the first to describe the new experience, but above all because it had to do with sexuality, and because one was then an adult. And one could get married. I still remember the first girl to menstruate. It was Ilse Bange. The girls trembled with envy and excitement. A great state of agitation: Who would be next?

I went around feeling gloomy once again, I would never have such good fortune. All the others were "it" already. Again, they began to question and torment me. Then it occurred to me to deceive them all. Thus, I arrived at school one morning, beaming. "It" was there. After lessons, I described the symptoms to the girls, symptoms I knew well because my girlfriends had often described them to me and the others.

And I was forced to uphold that lie for ten years, in many countries and among strange customs, and it caused me many a worry.

It could not be overlooked: I was growing a beard. Hella Langendorf said so, and kissed me because it scratched her like a man's beard. The whole class enjoyed this, and I was very popular once more. Long blond hairs grew on my upper lip, a new worry and a source of grief. I fought the unwanted ornament with scissors, until I noticed that the hairs only grew back all the more quickly and became darker and more visible.

We seldom played any longer. Circles were now established, and we visited one another with our needlework, especially before Christmas. We did but little work, and talked when it grew dark, in low voices, relating any number of revolting, obscene jokes about the mystery of the sexes.

Ilse had found a book about human sexuality in her mother's cupboard. She brought this treasure to school, and it was passed from hand to hand. On the days our circle met, we read aloud from it to one another. The Bible, too, had to serve our purpose. We soon knew all the passages by heart, and it was certainly not the psalms that we consulted repeatedly. Hella's Bible even fell open at a certain passage when it was opened, a sign of how often those particular verses were read.

The regional Ducal Secondary Boys' School stood opposite ours, both on municipal property. The whole building was built in a cheerful old-fashioned style, an agreeable contrast to our modern redbrick building. We girl pupils were expected to ignore their building. In the past, we had spun the traditional threads between the girls' school and the secondary school for boys, but now many a tender note was exchanged with the seventh-grade boys. Our interest in those strange creatures with the short hair increased. I say *our*, although my interest was very superficial, as may be imagined. The girls stared at the boys as though they were some kind of peculiar animals about whose habits strange tales circulated among us. We forgot that they were the friends of our youth, our brothers and cousins, and regarded them as an odd race that we observed with delighted dread. In the mornings, before lessons, the "experiences" of the day before were exchanged with proud satisfaction. Pfeiffer had greeted Lotte six times, and Herr Bode had met Lene seven times. Rendezvous were planned to which one went hesitantly in order to exchange kisses of first, shy love with the boys. I, unfortunately, never had such a tender relationship, and if I seemed to watch the other girls with calm smiling scorn, secretly I very much wanted such an adventure, naturally, only so as to be able to join in when the others flaunted their relationships like old, seasoned cocottes.

The two old spinsters, our teachers, warned us quite openly about the evils of men, and we were proud to have tamed the beasts with whom we were "walking out at the moment" so well. We met our protectors on the ice, and they performed many chivalrous duties. For us, they were representatives of a strange world that we loved and admired, and we were pleased if we were able to fulfill one of their wishes.

That was the natural reaction that had to result from this enforced estrangement of the sexes. Only coeducation can give us morally free, better human beings. It alone polishes off the corners, softens the boisterous nature of boys, and enlivens the serene nature of girls in an agreeable manner.

My favorite subject, physical education, all at once became my passion. This happened in the following way. We were exercising in the municipal gymnasium. The equipment, which today I only vaguely remember, seemed to me then to be the epitome of perfection. I enjoyed being in the gym. Scant light fell through the tall narrow windows, for it first had to pass through the green treetops of the neighboring garden before it shone serenely and mildly into the gym. It was afternoon, and the twilight that tempts those in love to behave foolishly lay over the gym. After doing some exercises, we had been allowed to dance, because the girls had pleaded to do so. The teacher was called away for a moment, but that did not bother us; we continued to dance in an ever wilder rhythm.

When the teacher returned, we were doing climbing exercises. I led the second team, and when I stepped forward to demonstrate the exercise, my strength abandoned me. I panted with exertion, and a strange heaviness lay over my limbs. At last, I regained control of myself and made a second attempt. I wrapped my legs around the pole and put my hands on it but could not pull myself up. Then Erna's hands pushed me up and my hands and feet grasped the pole in wilder and wilder efforts, until my strength deserted me. A hot, hitherto unknown, intoxicatingly pleasant feeling shook me, a shudder ran through my body, and weakly, I slid down to the ground.

The pleasant relaxation I felt at first was soon pushed aside by deep fear. What was that? Had something inside of me torn? Although I felt no pain, I was weary and shattered. I felt ashamed and looked shyly around me, but luckily none of the girls had noticed my strange behavior.

I felt this feeling often. It came unexpectedly when I ran quickly or lifted heavy loads, but mostly when I was climbing, however, always unconsciously and without my provoking it. One time, this feeling overcame me when I was having my teeth checked by the only female dentist in our town. The pain caused the feeling. From then on, I liked going to the dentist, until the large bills for my repeated visits began to arrive and caught Papa's attention. Of course, that put an end to that "sport."

So the last day of school arrived, and without great emotion, I accepted words of advice and my certificate from the hand of the old headmaster. Then a chorale followed, and a feigned thank-you to the teachers, and the school doors closed behind me for the last time.

The year after my schooling ended was one of the most pleasant in my life. Although I still had needlework lessons to continue my education, they were given by the learned teacher whom I liked very much, and thus were bearable. All in all, I did not do very much during this period. Mama would have liked to include me in the housework, but I always managed to free myself from it, and Papa's attempts to interest me in the lumber trade failed constantly. However, the newly arrived lots of wood did interest me. When we received a raft of fir trees, I loved to dream of the mountainous forest home of the trees, and the old twisted oak-tree trunks made me wonder how many generations they might have provided shade for. There my interest ended; the technicalities on which the wood trade hinges could not kindle my interest. Thus, Papa, who was by no means patient, left it at that, and set me free. Our business had become so small that he was well able to run it on his own. The unhappy financial situation of my father's business gradually became clear to me, too. I understood what it meant and asked no more clergymen what a mortgage was. Thus time passed with serious worries for us all. Papa was only able to maintain his business with an effort, by covering one promissory note with another. The profits were barely enough for our daily needs; they were almost completely swallowed up by the mortgage payments and interest on loans.

My playmates, who had started school a year later than I had, still went to school. I thus lost sight of my classmates, except for Hilde. I was bound to her by neighborly friendship, which on her part was to some extent fueled by self-interest, for she needed my help with her written homework. At this time, a house near the marketplace changed hands. The new owners, ducal officials who were from out of town, paid us a visit and brought along their daughter, a sweet, fresh girl of thirteen. Emma was to join school only in the winter term, and so we became close friends for the remainder of the summer term. The girl was a pretty child, with a fresh face framed by unruly black hair, and a healthy well-developed body. I felt very attracted to her. I would not have been able to say what it was about her that I liked so much, but for her sake I played games, which, from the height of my fifteen years, I ridiculed as "calf-like." I was entirely captivated by her. At that time, I did not understand the reason for the attraction; today, I am of the opinion that the child attracted me erotically. I was very fond of her. I remember a scene from July of that year. I awoke rather early and stretched out luxuriously in my bed, thinking about visiting Emma later on. She was surely still sleeping at this hour. I began to think of how she must look now, in her rumpled bed, her black hair tangled around her sleeping face, her arms uncovered, lying lightly on the blanket. And while I was thinking this, a wonderful feeling overcame me. I became restless; I wanted to go there. I imagined what would happen then. I would approach her bed quietly and kiss her awake. My vision became so clear that I saw how she stretched out her hand to me, drunken with sleep, and I thought I heard her protesting sleepily, "Please leave me be, I'm still so sleepy."

I remember another thing. One afternoon, I was lying lazily in the grass at the back of the wood yard. The bees were buzzing around me, and I found it entertaining to watch the butterflies flying from flower to flower, or the gnats dancing in the air. I was indulging in the secret vice of smoking cigarettes and amusing myself by blowing cigarette smoke on the swarms of gnats from time to time, and watching them fly apart in confused fright.

I was clearly remembering the pleasant dreams that I had once again succumbed to when all at once I heard a frightened voice calling my name from nearby. I hid the cigarette and jumped up. Emma came toward me with a deathly frightened face. She was pale and shaking. She seemed very ill, and she was so ashamed! I asked her what the matter was. At first, she did not want to say, but then it came out. Her first menstruation had frightened this ignorant child terribly. I reassured her, and we lay on the grass, chatting.

At night, I often had wild dreams now, to which my daytime thoughts could find no connection. I lay in bed, and beautiful women with brown hair and dark eyes bent over me. They wore no clothes, and they all obeyed me. They kissed me and allowed me to kiss them. New delights rippled through me, and unknown sensations whipped up all my vitality. When I awoke in the morning after such dreams, I felt tired and enervated.

The old doubts began anew. Whatever could I be? Boy or girl? If I was a girl, why were my breasts not growing? Why did I alone remain childish and undeveloped? Why did I not suffer from that "illness" that I found nauseating and dreadful, but wished for as a clear indication of my sexual designation? If I was a boy, why, then, this girl's name? All the deep suffering, which I had thought was behind me, began again and tormented me dreadfully.

Why did my parents not speak to me about this? A wild desperation and determination to know the truth took hold of me. Hundreds of times, I determined to ask my father and my mother, but time and again, my courage failed me.

My inhibitions about speaking to my parents are surely incomprehensible to many. It was the result of my upbringing. Not that we were forbidden to speak of sexual matters; but in our parents' home, not even the slightest reference to sexual matters was ever made. That is why it was quite impossible for me to ask my parents about what was depressing me. I really do not know what my parents must have thought when I failed to begin menstruating. My mother may have been seriously worried; my father shrank from the fuss.

Business became worse and worse. The worries at home became ever greater. My parents decided to have me trained for an occupation. Quite against my inclinations and without asking me about my wishes, they concluded an agreement with an acquaintance in a large town in Thuringia, according to which I was to enter a banking house. My training began on September 1. I suffered the torture of homesickness, grew very thin, and lost my fresh complexion. My home and the distant gray house seemed to me, in the glow of youthful memory, like a lost paradise.

A cold, which seriously weakened me, led my superior, Herr Werder, to send me to a doctor, who examined my lungs, wrote a few lines to my superior, and gave the letter to me. Herr Werder then wrote to Bergheim, and as a result of this correspondence my parents brought me back home. My superior's young daughter told me that the doctor had written that I was consumptive. This frightened me very much, but nevertheless I arrived cheerfully in Bergheim and was only glad to have escaped the despised occupation.

Mama took my illness so casually that I found this indifference extremely disconcerting. Indeed, I was appalled. I added this new reproach to the pile of others that I held against her. Only many years later, after we had at last spoken to each other openly, did she show me that letter. My superior wrote that unfortunately he would have to do without my services, as my lungs had become weak. For this reason, and because of my frailty, which, in the opinion of the doctor, was apparent in my unusual lack of physical development, I should first gain strength in the fresh mountain air of my hometown for a year before rejoining the business a year later. And, by the way, it would then be a great pleasure, and so forth.

So Mother knew what had fooled the doctor and, for that reason, was quite unworried. At that time, though, I felt her calm as coldness, and that merely increased the distance between us. I was of an age when, for young people, love and tenderness are as necessary as daily bread. The fermentation and changes during puberty make love so necessary for those on the verge of adulthood.

From that period, I can still remember dreaming of women who played in wide waters, soft white bodies, whose curving lines I saw breaking the surface of the blue waves and disappearing again like a vision. On the seashores stood strange trees.

This dream first came to me when I slept in the gray house again, after my absence. It returned often then, and was so vivid that I attempted to draw it. In the end, I came to believe that it was a scene that I had experienced in a former life.

Only a few memories of Bergheim during this period have remained in my mind, due to the constant struggle with oppressive problems of all kinds. The approaching ruin was always before my parents' eyes. My mother had but one wish: that my father might be spared the sight of the sad end of his once large fortune. The lack of money became chronic, the demands for the promissory notes piled up, and it was barely possible to manage from one day to the next.

My father's illness grew steadily worse. In the spring, an operation became necessary. Afterward, the invalid grew visibly weaker. My siblings were called home; we spent night and day by his bedside. Then the end came.

A day in June, the air heavy with the sweet scent of blossoms. From the garden, the fragrance of linden trees invaded the sickroom through wide-open windows. The air was clear and calm. The sound of the trees trembling in the light summer breeze entered the room with a soft murmur. A dreamy splashing could be heard from the fountain.

I had relieved my sisters of their vigil. The invalid lay quietly; one could scarcely hear him breathing. After I had renewed the icy compress, I drew a chair up to the window and looked longingly out at the garden. I took up my book, a tale by Gerstäcker. I had not been reading for long when I looked up. An eerie silence hung in the room. Very quietly, I approached the bed. I could see no movement of my father's chest. His heart stood still. I had the idea to pluck a feather from the coverlet and hold it to the dying man's mouth, for I wanted to be certain before I alarmed the others. The feather did not move. First, I called my brother. Then we both went to our mother and prepared her. Everyone wept; I, however, did not, but deep dismay took hold of me when I saw death for the first time.

Now followed the formalities, the necessary business that is the responsibility of mourners. On the second day, he was laid out in his coffin. The death chamber was completely filled with flowers, and more kept arriving. Then came the funeral. Later, when the carriage rolled along the road, I listened to the muffled noise disappearing into the distance, and a feeling akin to solemnity overcame me. A weight was removed from my soul, and I breathed a sigh of relief. Soon after, I removed from my heart and my mind that man who should have been dear to me but who had merely given me life and then not bothered about me any further. Was the kind of life I led, torn by worries and by doubts about the most essential component of human nature, a gift for which I owed my father thanks?

For us, the bereaved family, a period of abject poverty followed. The business was closed, and the gray house became the property of others. An occupation had to be found for me that would quickly enable me to earn a living. Mama heard from a friend that a fashion shop in Sellberg was looking for an apprentice. She wrote to them and received an answer. After a short consultation, an agreement was reached. The apprenticeship was to last for two years, after which I was to be further employed and given a salary.

I was quite distraught in view of these prospects, but nothing more suitable was to be found at the time. August 1, the day on which we had to vacate the house, drew nearer, and so we settled on July 15 as our day of departure.

During the final days, I walked around as though laboring under a dream. The parting from my home was made easier for me by the fact that I was going to a strange town where no one knew my secret.

My mother accompanied me on my train journey. Upon arrival in the big, noisy town, we asked directions by foot to the shop of Ludwig Werner. Our travel funds would not cover transport in the town. Finally, we found the shop. When we entered and saw the coldly glittering splendor of this big town palace of business, my heart contracted with fear; the many strange people made me feel so lonely that I clung to my mother like a child. We had to wait for some time. When Herr Werner came at last, he looked at me, wide-eyed. When I then answered his questions, he said, "My, my! You have the voice of a man." When he saw me recoil, he added jovially, "Well, that doesn't matter. I hope that you will make all the stronger an impression on the customers."

In the evening, my mother took her leave, I was allowed to accompany her to the train.

The next morning, a salesgirl showed me my duties. I had been assigned to the woolen-goods warehouse. First thing in the morning, I was to dust off the cash register, next to which stood the seats of the cashier and the manager. Every Friday, their desks were scrubbed, which was, of course, also my task. On Saturdays, such tasks could not be done, as the weekly market took place on that day, and more customers came, which meant more work for the staff.

The Werner Company employed about fifty people. Besides me, there were three other female apprentices, one of them in the finery department, and five male apprentices. The work of the apprentices in such large shops consists mostly of cleaning the premises and other menial tasks that have little to do with actually learning the business.

We had to dust, pack boxes, run errands, scrub, and clean the metal parts of the showcases, the stairs, and so forth. That was not particularly pleasant work, especially in winter. We shivered with cold in the early hours of the morning when we stood in front of the shop door, cleaning the brass rods of the windows. Our fingers became swollen and turned purple, and our chilblains often burst open.

Only now and again during the Christmas season were the female apprentices allowed to do the actual work of selling. The rest of the time, they were mostly kept busy tidying up and scouring.

Of course, I have one particular business in mind, the one in which I was trained. But the conditions can well be generalized. By the way, jobs with the Werner Company were very much sought after. There was a waiting list, as the firm was considered to be a particularly good one that treated its employees well.

A printed list of rules and regulations with twenty-five sections: "It is forbidden to the staff to . . ." saw to it that order prevailed. Among others, there was a rule: "Relationships between members of staff will not be tolerated, nor is it permitted to have relations with staff members of a competing firm." Despite these strict rules, there were many dark corners in the building that served as places to "smooch." When I was sent on an errand to the cellar or the attic, I sometimes disturbed couples who then sprang apart.

The entire staff had to obey the rules. The only exception was the window dresser, Herr Berger, for whom some exceptions were tolerated. "I am an artist and cannot bow to this philistine yoke," he explained to the owner. He portrayed his status as an artist outwardly, too, by wearing long curls and a velvet jacket. All newly hired salesgirls went into raptures over him, a beginners' ailment that every "new girl" had to go through.

When Herr Berger was nervous, and he usually was on Monday mornings, not a loud word was to be spoken in his vicinity. Even the boss tried to muffle his loud bass until it became the lightest of purrs. This privileged position of window dressers can be explained by the fact that people who are skilled in this job are few and far between and are becoming ever rarer, because the demands on this trade are immense. It is not enough today to pile up various articles in the shop window; the eyes of the big-city dwellers must be captivated by modern symphonies of color, fabulous clouds of silk. Some shops pay window dressers salaries that can be compared with those of a private councillor.

There is traditional enmity between stock clerks and window dressers on the days when the latter work. The window dresser roams through the stockrooms with a critical eye, looking for the most attractive things to display in the shop windows. The girls, however, do not like to give these things to him, as the goods suffer in the windows and can later be sold only at a reduced price. Those are very tiring days, indeed! Herr Berger worked very quickly, and although, as a rule, he was very friendly, on those days the apprentices were bawled out countless times, or had their ears boxed if they did not understand his intentions quickly enough.

Ever since that time, whenever I pass by a particularly attractively dressed shop window, I always have to think of the tears that splendor must have cost, and when I see the shining metal decorations in shops, I think of the poor female apprentices with their hands frozen blue, polishing away in the early hours of the morning.

In large shops with extensive staff, there is naturally no lack of intrigue. One person puts all her effort into her work, another is lazy, and another works only when the boss is watching. The ones who are to be pitied the most are the female apprentices. There were fifty members of staff when I entered the business; thus I had fifty superiors, all of whom thought that they had a special claim to my personal services. The apprentice who was released by me from the unenviable position of "youngest" merrily ordered me about along with the swarm of others, and because I was as yet unable to find my way around the hierarchy and would have liked to please everyone, I naturally managed to do nothing properly.

Oh, how very unhappy I felt. But I comforted myself with the thought that all the other female apprentices had been through the same thing. Each of the salesgirls must have had similar experiences, so I hardly had a special reason to complain.

One must consider that it was not only the unfamiliar humiliation of my position that weighed upon me, but above all the degradation and torment that arose out of my particular nature. The jokes I was forced to endure affected me much more cruelly when they were made by my superiors than the teasing of my comrades in school had done. The head saleswoman, who had a poor memory for names, at first always called me to her with the words, "the one with the man's voice is to come to me." This invariably caused a burst of whinnying laughter, just like the friendly suggestion by one of the salesmen that I should be carefully examined to see whether I was not a man in disguise. A few of the more fanciful young men imagined how pleasant it must be to live as the only man among so many girls. They grinned and stared at me lustfully.

How frightened I felt when I was forced to listen to such talk! I lived like a harassed animal.

The hair on my face gave rise to mockery as well. Innumerable jokes were made about it. One day at dinner, they left a mustache holder on my plate.

Among the customers were numerous peasants and laborers. I trembled when I had to ask one of them what he wanted. They stared at me, whispering to one another and laughing loudly. My resulting reluctance to serve customers was taken by my boss for laziness, and he was therefore not particularly delighted with his new apprentice. When the staff got wind of this, my position became entirely unbearable.

Perhaps I would have gotten over all of this if my every attempt to get close to and win the confidence of the female staff, to which I was, after all, considered to belong, had not been thwarted. I think the staff of this establishment was above average, for Herr Werner carefully chose the most capable and decent people, and it was considered a recommendation in business circles at that time to have worked for him.

The female staff was accommodated in the manager's home so that their moral conduct could be watched over, but also for economic reasons.

I slept in a room with three young girls. This caused much unpleasantness. I retired at the early hour of ten o'clock in the evening so as not to have to undress in front of the others. In the mornings, however, dressing together could not be avoided. While the others unabashedly opened their shirts to wash their chests, I hardly dared bare my neck and arms. At first, the girls took this for shame and shyness about undressing before strangers. When, after eight days, I still showed no signs of bowing to the habits of the others, they were surprised and encouraged me. Finally, they took me for an utterly slovenly wench, and I had to endure many ugly remarks because of my imagined filthiness. Finally, my colleagues said they would go to our superior if I did not break the habit of being dirty. No one wanted to share a room with me any longer.

I was helpless, desperate. The abnormal circumstances under which I lived, the constant fear of being found out, had caused a hypersensitive feeling of shame or, rather, anxiety to develop in me. What should I do? I brooded but found no way out. That evening, I went earlier than usual to our room, where I always washed myself in the evenings, in the dark. Absentmindedly, I had forgotten to lock the door. A passing colleague heard the splashing of water and called the others, who, at the announcement that the "dirty one" was washing herself, came running, tore open the door, and, a crowd of Psyches, with their lamps in their hands, stared at me, poor half-naked Cupid. Frightened and ashamed, I threw myself onto my bed. What now? Discovery would surely follow. But when all remained silent, I dared look up. All the girls had left, with the exception of a large blond girl who had begun work a few days before. She sat on the edge of the bed stroking my hair and saying in her soft southern German accent, "You poor little thing, you needn't be ashamed because you're so skinny! So that's the reason that you don't want to wash in the mornings?" Trembling, I nodded, yes.

Everyone had seen me, so now I washed in the mornings like the others, and went to bed later, as they did. They only thought I was thin and as lacking in breasts as a ten-year-old. They noticed nothing more. Why should they have had greater anatomical knowledge than the doctor who had thought me consumptive?

After the secretiveness was over, my relations with the girls improved. I could be of use to some of them by correcting their love letters, or thinking of new, more expressive phrases for those letters, putting words of foreign origin into German, and writing letters for those who sought new positions. During the day, there was little opportunity to chat, so the talkative girls gossiped for ages in their beds at night. Here, too, besides the events of the day, sexual matters were most often discussed. Because none of the girls had had sexual relations with a man yet, the unknown territory was all the more appealing. Each of them obliged us with her views. Jokes that had been picked up somewhere were told so that we could almost die laughing at the only half-understood punch lines. Bodies and busts were compared. Naturally, I did not take part in this comparison; the others understood, "because I had nothing to compare." Even if I did not participate in the comparison, these beauty competitions held great appeal for me. I could become so enthusiastic about beautiful figures that I trembled with excitement.

I thought this pleasure in the female body was a purely aesthetic joy. The thought of sexual attraction scarcely occurred to me.

Gradually, I was losing the feeling that I was a boy altogether. I had read in a pseudoscientific book that in anemic and poorly developed girls, menstruation did not begin before the twenties. Thus, I came to believe sometimes that I was an abnormal girl. The fact that I was more attracted by female bodies than by men I attributed to an artistic taste.

This auto-suggestion favorably influenced my relations with my companions. I was more relaxed, which resulted in their being friendlier toward me. I still remember some of the scandals we talked about. One day, it leaked out that one of the [unmarried] salesmen was going to be a father. We were very indignant about the degenerate girl and viewed the young man with lascivious curiosity. We continued to speak of it and about how the young man might have managed it, after we had gone to bed.

Although we knew a little about the nature of the relations between the sexes, the little we knew was so muddled that we could not picture it. In any case, we feared men, as they all seemed to us to be brutes, each one of them a Bluebeard, even the husband, who surely raped his wife anew daily. Every woman seemed a saint, forced to submit to such a greedy monster.

I also remember when a prostitute who was known all over town made a purchase in our shop. We were divided into two parties then: the one despised her; the other, to which I belonged, pitied the unfortunate creature, who was so poor that she had to suffer the torture of daily debauchery. Of course, the girls did not use that expression, but a much coarser one that I cannot repeat here. We were of the opinion then that women had to bear all the pain and suffering. This was in agreement with my dreams, in which women served me, and I was their severe master.

I also remember that one young girl had a tumor on her breast. The doctor prescribed massages, and as I was particularly clever with my hands, I had to do it. This always greatly aroused me. Those amorous dreams became more and more frequent, and that girl played an ever greater role among the figures in my dreams. I kissed and caressed her, naturally only in my dreams. I did have a desire to kiss her during the massages, but I was fearful and controlled myself. The impulse to kiss came over me often during this time. My dreams, which had formerly been of a more brutal character, now contained a tender premonition of a true love life.

We were also surprised to hear about lesbian love then. We admired this love, which we thought was more delicate and without pain, but we hardly believed in it. It occurred to me that I alone perhaps felt like a lesbian. Then again, I pushed the idea firmly aside.

We often spoke in the evenings of "the habits of gentlemen." An instinctive revulsion, probably fear of venereal disease, prevented the girls from using the same towels as the young men had used to dry their hands.

The girls' semi-ignorance stood in contrast to the disgusting cynicism of the salesmen. They told the dirtiest stories, boasted of their sexual adventures, and loved telling unambiguous tales in the presence of the girls, who suffered greatly from the embarrassment of only partially understanding. Today, these stories seem to me like the perverse deeds of sadists or exhibitionists!

By the way, the young people in more educated circles are often merely more refined, but no better than the lower classes.

Although I was spared quite a few humiliations because of my improved relations with the girls, my position entailed so much that was offensive that my original distaste for the trade that had been forced upon me became even greater. Probably only a few people have an inkling of the great effort that this occupation takes.

So often, one speaks of actors who must laugh on stage, although their hearts be as sad as can be; one writes and reads tear-jerking tales of pitiful extras and dancers who must smile, although one of their loved ones is lying ill at home. But not a single person considers the fact that the faces of salesgirls, too, are often only a mask for suffering and sorrow. And while the actress is only forced to feign a strange life that she does not live for a few hours on stage, salesgirls are unfortunate creatures who may not remove their masks, day in and day out, from morning till night.

A salesgirl must remain friendly, even when treated in the most ill-mannered way. The greatest demands are made on her patience. The inconsiderateness of women who are eager to buy often knows no boundaries. Before making a purchase, many women are in the habit of asking the price in ten different shops in order to compare them and do not consider that the sales assistant or salesgirl who served them is reprimanded—and, in some shops, even fined—for every customer who leaves the shop without buying anything.

Poverty is especially great among salesgirls in big cities. The following true story was told at that time: a gentleman in Cologne on the Rhein hired a salesgirl. "I will pay you twenty-five marks a month." "But I cannot live on that," the girl protested. "That is your problem, dear child. Besides, you are only engaged in my shop during the day(!!)."

One of the apprentices who knew Bergheim and my family was more polite to me than the others were. I was very grateful to him for that. Unfortunately, the friendship did not last for long because the young man, probably misled by my comradely trust, became insolent, and one day when we were working in a cellar together, made advances on me. I boxed his ears soundly, but our friendship was, of course, finished after that.

A minor thunderstorm was brewing over me once again. I had been working for Werner for about six months when the washerwoman who took care of my things began to say that everything could not be right with me, because as long as she had been washing my things, and so on and so forth . . .

In order to avoid such dangerous discussions, I changed washerwomen every eight weeks from then on. I do not know whether anyone can understand that this so very unimportant, even ridiculous, affair seemed to me to be a tragic aspect of my life. How much time this irrelevant matter consumed. How much laughter I had to endure because of it, how much scorn! I felt outrage against a fate that had imposed so much inconvenience on me.

At that time, I suffered from religious doubts, doubts about the balance of social justice. The lowliness of my rank nauseated me. I wanted to liberate myself but knew not how. I knew only that I wanted to learn, to learn a great deal, because I believed that only knowledge and skills could lift me up from the position I then held.

An almost fanatical longing to acquire knowledge took hold of me. To go to university: all my dreams revolved around that goal. Every graduate seemed to me like a demigod. Medicine attracted me above all. In it and through it, I hoped to finally gain clarity about myself.

My desire to learn increased until it became pathological. I felt a genuine hunger for education, I wanted to gain knowledge, whatever it was. Business knowledge would have been fine with me, something abstract that could have torn me from the concrete conditions of my daily work. The male apprentices seemed enviable, because they at least had their commercial schools. They learned English, French, stenography, and commercial arithmetic.

I took out my old schoolbooks with zeal, went over old ground, things I had learned long before, and spent every free minute writing down my thoughts as essays on wrapping paper, the margins of old newspapers, or whatever happened to be at hand.

My colleagues drew my attention to an obscure lending library that charged very low prices. There were no scholarly books there, so I gained cheap wisdom from novels.

Naturally, my enthusiasm for the business suffered from these diverse interests, but Herr Wagner graciously overlooked this. I held a modest position of trust with him; I translated and answered any foreign correspondence and was the interpreter when foreigners came into the shop. He paid me for these small services by taking me to a literary society several times to listen to lectures. The memory of those lectures is the highlight of that period. This took place three or four times. I won Herr Wagner over most of all because I worked with his sons, one in seventh grade, and one in fifth. I wrote their compositions and helped them with their English and French. I enjoyed doing that because it made me feel very important. In addition, I was excused from work during those hours.

In order to get some benefit from my work in spite of my clumsiness as a salesgirl, I was sent to the alterations department on a trial basis. It had become very difficult for me to sell anything. It went against the grain for me to persuade people to buy things they did not like or did not really need, but a capable businessman must be able to do that. I found acting in this way unprincipled.

Thus, I came to the sewing room. At first I had feared the work, for I remembered my clumsiness at handiwork all too well from my school days; however, this kind of sewing was fairly easy for me. I only had to backstitch long seams on a machine, the mechanics of which I soon grasped.

It is not rare for men to do machine sewing.

It was all the same to me what they kept me busy with during the day, for I regarded that time as empty hours that kept me from my favorite work, books. In the evenings, I found a new lease on life. When the shop was closed, the young women gathered in a communal sitting room and did handiwork and chatted. I worked and often read aloud to them. When the others went out walking on Sunday afternoons, I sat in the lifeless rooms and read.

Among the books, which I borrowed from the library, were brochures on women's rights and feminism. These new views filled me with enthusiasm, because they were entirely in accord with my own legal concepts. I thought the demands were justified, exactly in agreement with my feelings, as though I had written down my own opinions. I felt the physical and mental equal of men and saw no reason why they should be privileged and have better chances of getting an education than I, and other women, had. That was what I had thought for a long time, and finally found it clearly expressed. Enthusiastically, I spent hours lecturing my colleagues until they, too, were converted to my point of view.

After having worked in the shop for about a year, I was sent for further training to a branch of the firm in a small provincial town in Saxony. The old suffering began anew under changed circumstances. But this time, I was able to win the confidence of the staff more quickly. The town had a public library from which I borrowed many books, but not all good ones, however, for these libraries are often the dumping grounds for completely useless stuff that people want to rid their bookshelves of. Some of the staff at the shop subscribed to a daily newspaper, and because I was very obliging, they most willingly let me read it, too.

At that time, one of those shattering events took place that bring immeasurable disaster to entire regions. The newspapers reported all the details, and appeals were made for donations. In view of the misery, everything was needed, from money to secondhand clothing.

The misery of the homeless masses seized my imagination. They were surely poorer than I was, and how I wanted to help them! But what could I do? My monthly pocket money amounted to three marks; that was enough to buy the paper, pens, and stamps I needed, but not to donate even the smallest sum to the unfortunate victims of the catastrophe in A. Even then, I said to myself that although the pennies that the poor contribute to those who are even poorer are ethically more worthy, the talers from the rich have greater purchasing power and are therefore to be preferred. So activity like that was more than my small resources could bear. And to ask others, rich people, to give me money, that was a difficult task, for who would entrust money to me, an unknown salesgirl? So I had to make do with collecting articles of warm clothing. I set to work, asking my male and female colleagues for old clothing, and begging them to ask all their acquaintances for such things as well. Thus, I received quite a few articles of clothing, which, however, were not all in the best condition; many were torn and soiled.

At the sight of this, for the first time in my life, I lost my loathing of the needle and female handiwork. I had no time during the day, so I had to make use of the nights. I sat in the poorly heated sittingroom until three o'clock in the morning or later, sewing as long as my stiff fingers could hold the needle. On other evenings, I washed the soiled clothing. That was the most difficult task, as I had no washing equipment.

Housewives will understand that the undergarments I washed with unskilled hands, piece by piece in my hand basin, did not always come out spotless. The unaccustomed work and the bending weakened me considerably. Often I only went to bed in the early hours of the morning, shaking with cold and with pains in my hands. Finally, the branch manager forbade me to do this work. After that I did it in secret, and my colleagues did not betray me. The nights belonged to me; I could do as I liked then. Of course, I was fatigued the next day; after all, I was only seventeen years old, and young people need their sleep.

One evening, a new saleswoman told our fortunes with cards. She prophesied that I would receive a letter, and that my pious deeds would bring me good luck. I laughed at her superstition; I would have preferred her help. What I was doing was certainly not a pious deed, but rather the natural result of my social conscience.

In a hidden corner stood my collecting box. Every morning, I added the pieces that had been finished the night before to the other things, and was pleased that my stocks were increasing. When the box was almost full, I wrote to a member of the relief committee, asking where the nearest collection point was.

I had expected to receive a short printed or written note, with instructions on where to send my collection of "antiquities," as the young salesmen jokingly called them, and was therefore not a little surprised to receive a thick letter, closed with a large seal. The letter was most kind. After thanking me for my letter, the gentleman expressed his surprise at receiving support from someone in my position, and inquired who had encouraged me to contribute. He wrote that he would be pleased to hear from me soon.

The letter was passed from hand to hand and duly admired. The fortune-teller spoke up and said that the letter had arrived, and the rest would follow. In any case, the letter had made me happy. Messages from higher social strata were always associated with purer, more elevated intellectual pursuits in my mind.

Some days later, I replied to the gentleman that I had made the decision to collect the donations on my own, and informed him that I had dispatched the box.

This led to further correspondence, in which City Councillor Herr O. asked me how I came to be in my position, and whether I was happy there, or whether I had a wish. If so, then I was to write to him.

In my reply, I wrote to Herr O. of my childhood, but of course nothing of my secret, which I fearfully hid. I had no wish that could be fulfilled, other than for books. I wanted to learn, nothing more than to learn.

Eight days later, I received a package of good books, which the city councillor had chosen for me from his own library, and with it a friendly, encouraging letter. Did I have a particular interest as far as the studies I had mentioned were concerned? He had guessed my dearest wish: I wanted to attend university. Of course, I was not to build up my hopes, but he wanted to try to use his influence to help me.

I was in seventh heaven and walked about in a dream. What good fortune! Religious terror took hold of my soul, and I swore to myself that if I was helped, I would use all my powers to help others. In my enthusiasm, I wrote to my new benefactor. I told him that it was my dearest wish to study medicine, and how I had dreamed of this even as a child. I also wrote him of my childish scientific experiments, of my attempts to dissect dead rats and mice. How marvelous it must be to arrive as a rescuer at the moment of greatest need. But political economy, too, was also of great interest to me.

His kind answer ended with the friendly words: "By the way, my dear young friend, I am eager to make your acquaintance. You have such a quick mind and an understanding such as I have never before met in a woman. I hope we will be able to work together successfully later on."

At this time, I heard from a colleague that there was to be a lecture on the so-called rights of women in the business association to which he belonged. The speaker was a well-known reactionary, quite an unimportant person, whose only strength lay in nosing out the weaknesses of his esteemed fellow citizens. I knew how this man would deal with the matter that was so dear to me.

Dismayed, I turned to Herr O. and asked his advice.

He himself could not have anything to do with matters of this kind, he wrote back, but he directed me to a friend of his son's who lived in a large neighboring town. This gentleman had often demonstrated his interest in women's rights. I contacted him immediately, and received reassurances that he would come to our town on the aforementioned evening.

The big evening came. With the permission of my superior, I picked the gentleman up from the station. His readiness to undertake the journey surprised me; later, I learned that he had done so at the request of my paternal friend, who wanted to hear a firsthand opinion of me.

People looked up, surprised when I entered the room with the stranger.

A spirited debate, which ended in victory for the women's party, filled the evening. This was the first public meeting in which I participated. I felt entirely in my element. The speaker of my party seemed to me, in his victorious eloquence, like a demigod, whom I soon wished to emulate. I would have liked to join in the debate, but I refrained, for I did not wish to further irritate my boss, and because I feared that it would discredit the cause if a person as unimportant as I was joined in. The discussion lasted until midnight.

We parted that night with a handshake. My fellow workers prophesied an extremely unpleasant atmosphere for me the following morning. But all were in agreement that they had never experienced so enjoyable an evening.

The next morning, there was a big scene. Herr Mueller wanted to fire the female apprentice, "the green thing, who dared to have an opinion that differed from that of so many rich and older people."

It took many weeks for the storm to die down.

When I pass through that town today on my travels, my former boss greets me with a beaming smile, invites me to be his guest, and introduces me to every traveling salesman who arrives. He takes him into a corner and whispers to him: "And just think, Nora Body, you have heard of her, of course? What, everyone has heard of her! This Nora Body was once my apprentice, hard to believe, yes?"

The highlights in my life then were letters from my friends, especially those from the city councillor. I waited for them with almost as much suspense as a young man in love waits for letters from his beloved. He always wrote me kindly, and above all in such a noble manner that gratitude was not a burden, but a genuine joy. Few people know how to give. Some demand effusive thanks: others make taking impossible by refusing even the most modest thank-you, often the only service that the receiver of the gift can render in return. Herr O. proved to be ideally tactful in this matter. Each of his letters gave me moral support in those difficult times. Never did they create the impression that they were written by a patron to his protégé, but rather underlined the friendship in our relationship and almost gave the impression that he, the elder, should be grateful to the younger person. I owe him almost more for this noble and tactful behavior than for all his deeds.

One day, he wrote that it seemed to him imperative to meet me personally.

He chose a place nearby. A few days later, we met for the first time. In the course of our short conversation, my patron made a confession: the stipends that he had at his disposal only covered two years. I could not study medicine, since I lacked the necessary university entrance qualifications.

Although I could gain those qualifications by applying myself diligently for two years, there would have been little money left afterward for the years at university. I also wished to be in a position soon to support myself and my mother and to repay the sum received. After a short period of reflection on whether, in the end, studying philosophy might not be preferable, I decided that very same day on political economy.

Like every amateur who approaches this broad field, I hoped someday to make a contribution to solving social problems. Giving up the idea of studying medicine was a great disappointment, but because I am a very active person I became engrossed in my work and soon resigned myself to what could not be changed.

My mother placed massive, unexpected stumbling blocks in my path. She disliked the thought of my attending university. She also had experienced so much gloom in her eventful life that she was unable to believe in such good luck. Over and above that, it meant that the chances of my earning a living would recede too far into the future. For these reasons, she refused to grant me permission to attend university. Finally, she turned directly to Herr O. and asked for clarification. His reply, which arrived soon afterward, calmed her fears. In the letter, which I still have in my possession, he wrote:

"Whatever your daughter may take upon herself to do, she will always hold her own. We have here the opportunity to elevate her to the level where she belongs according to her abilities, and I believe your daughter shall one day occupy a position of responsibility where she will do you and us credit, contribute to the salvation of all women, and be a blessing to mankind."

After that, my mother no longer refused her permission. My apprenticeship contract was dissolved.

We had chosen Berlin as the place where I would attend university. On April 1, I arrived in the German capital. The train had to wait outside the entrance to the Potsdamer Bahnhof train station, because the tracks were all occupied. I sat, intolerably restless in my corner, drunk with the thought of being near this gigantic city with its innumerable opportunities for higher learning.

After overcoming various difficulties, I was admitted as a student. I shall pass over the details of the following period and only mention that I did not find my studies difficult, that the professors respected me, and that I was popular with my fellow students. The work caused me indescribable joy. I was liberated from my yoke, saved from the suffering! In the sphere of learning, my pains, worries, and doubts about my sex faded. The intellectual pursuits, which I took up with great enthusiasm, soothed my overstrained nerves, and I began to feel like a human being among other human beings.

Not like a person of equal value, but like someone who should be valued differently from the others.

I worked with veritable zeal. In my spare time, I wrote a series of articles on the subject "The Best Way of Organizing Charitable Societies." The articles were accepted for publication by a respected journal. Dr. M., an authority in the field, had asked incredulously, "What? A young girl of seventeen is supposed to have written these lines? Impossible. I do not think that any woman can possibly write like that." Similar things were often said to me. Therefore, there must be something specifically masculine about my intellectual activity, which women who write do not usually possess.

I should like to underline once again the view that I gained during my girlhood—in other words, from such a precise knowledge of women, one that other men can hardly gain. My thesis is: "Women are not inferior to men but, rather, different." They are certainly capable of achieving as much as men in scholarly endeavor, albeit in different ways. The only difference lies in the method.

In general, my articles were kindly received. Understandably, this encouraged me in my work and helped it along. I made all kinds of contacts, which seemed to me would be useful for my future.

I quickly became popular among the students. When judging female students, the aspects considered differ from those employed when assessing a salesgirl.

One of my fellow students asked me to participate in a public meeting. This was during the first weeks of my studies. The hall was overcrowded. The charged atmosphere, which the presence of so many people exudes, lay in the air. I did not approve of what the man at the lectern was saying. In a heated voice, and somewhat self-consciously, I joined the discussion. Lively applause proved that the manner in which I had dispatched the previous speaker pleased the crowd. I took the floor often that evening, and my initial inhibition faded more and more. Since that maiden speech, I have spoken at any number of public meetings in many different countries without feeling even a trace of stage fright.

In a students' group, I met a young American girl who was attending a lyceum in Berlin. She was particularly friendly to me and spoiled me with kindness. Her affection was rather odd in character. She loved waiting on me, carried my books, made me tea, and did me various other small services. When we went swimming together one day, she insisted on helping me get dressed, and I could hardly protect myself from her hands. "*I love you with all my heart,*" she said again and again "*and I feel for you in quite a different way from what I do for all my other comrades.*" [The words in italics are in English in the original.]

She was a hotly sensuous, passionate creature who, at the age of seventeen, carried her virginity like a heavy burden. She kissed me often and pressed my hands to her breasts in bursts of passion. She was happy if I left them there, or lightly stroked her, lovingly. I enjoyed doing this. She excited my senses to the point of wild ecstasy, which, however, was followed by a feeling of letdown, for my senses in the end remained unsatisfied.

By chance, she arrived at my rooms one afternoon when I was lying dressed on my bed. We spoke of the news of the day, but she was confused and unable to follow me. Her eyes darted about nervously. Suddenly, she threw herself on top of me, embraced me ardently and kissed me wildly. She spoke confused words that I did not understand. Her body jerked in hysterical convulsions. At first, I wanted to push her away, for I found her hysterics repulsive. In the end, I threw my arms around her and returned her kisses.

Without saying a word, she left. I was unable to work for the rest of that day. At night, I dreamed of her. I dreamed of possessing her.

But I dared make no attempt to fathom her feelings for me; I would undoubtedly have had to reveal my secret to her. I also believed that she was only attracted to women and that I would be repulsive to her as a man.

In reality, Harriet was a normal girl who had never felt attracted to women and who later made a normal marriage. It was the man in me to whom she instinctively felt physically attracted. This was due to the mysterious sexual drive to which she fell victim, as much as she tried with all the strength of her spirit to fight it.

From then on, I avoided her, for I began to be afraid of her. Her embraces made me weak, almost faint, and because I remained unsatisfied, I suffered from the wild impulses of my inflamed nerves. After scenes like that, I was always very excited. I felt the impulse to embrace the girl, to crush her to a pulp, to kill her. Then I was ashamed of my brutal impulses and avoided her.

Later I found a young girl, a Friesian, who was slavishly devoted to me. She loved me, felt boundless admiration for me and everything I did. She, too, kissed me often. However, I remained cool, as I was relieved to have escaped Harriet's sensual attacks. "I love your hands," she said one day. "Hit me! It must be a joy to be struck by such hands!"

I answered very brusquely, as I found such outpourings repulsive. After that, she cooled off. Then a vague longing for her presence awoke in me. I tried to draw her to me once again, attended gatherings where I would meet her, even walked up and down in front of her window. My erotic dreams focused on her for a while. But she was avoiding me. I soon gave up this unworthy role and returned all the more earnestly to my studies. With renewed enthusiasm, I took up my journalistic activities once more.

I wrote to Herr O. often and with pleasure. He asked a professor, who was tutoring me privately, about my progress. The professor replied: "As far as our Miss N. O. Body is concerned, in spite of her youth, her knowledge is very broad, and her faculties strikingly keen, both characteristics that are very seldom so highly developed in a young girl of her age." I was only informed of the contents of this letter after I had completed my studies.

A young Russian student was giving a tea party one evening. It was usually very cozy in her rooms, so I accepted her invitation. The discussions were very lively. We debated a philosophical question, and as the subject interested me, I often joined the debate.

A student from Hamburg who had joined our circle for the first time that evening lived in the same district as I did. Therefore, we walked home together through the warm summer's evening.

This companion was a tall girl with an intelligent expression and a perfect figure. She carried her splendid head, which was crowned with glorious blond braids, bent proudly back. Her blue eyes shone deeply. A hazy, devoted sensuousness lay over her being.

We walked arm in arm toward our neighborhood. Through our thin summer blouses, we felt the warmth of our bodies and the throbbing of our blood. I was excited, and she even more so. She said all manner of kind things about my essays, which she had read. But the conversation faltered again and again. At last we both fell silent. From time to time, she pressed my arm with hot, shy tenderness.

I accompanied her to her rooms. I did so from a feeling of natural chivalrousness toward the female sex, to which, in an odd combination, I felt both devoted and at the same time superior. Besides, I would certainly be better able to deal with potential improper advances by a man than shy Lucie would be. We parted, hoping to see each other soon.

When I awoke the next morning from restless dreams, I found a telegram announcing her visit that afternoon. She came, and we again took pleasure in each other's company. We became good friends.

When the summer holidays came around, at the invitation of her mother, I was her guest for several weeks. The time spent in Hamburg was extremely pleasant. The Lensteins' home displayed good taste. The furnishings were luxurious, but in no way ostentatious.

Lucie's father was traveling through Scandinavia, and her mother was an invalid, so we depended on one another a great deal.

From that time on, I kept a journal. After having written from my memory until here, I now have my journals at my disposal. I shall therefore relate the following on the basis of my notes.

Frau Lenstein was bedridden. I spent many an hour in her company, and I believe that she became genuinely fond of me. One day, she suggested that I move in with them. I would certainly find peace and quiet for my work in their home. No duties would be attached to this offer; if I would from time to time devote an hour of conversation to her or Lucie, they would regard this as a voluntarily granted kindness and accept it gratefully.

The two years during which I had received a stipend had passed, and my studies had progressed so far that I could continue them on my own, for I did not hanker after academic honors. This gracious invitation would have freed me from a serious worry, but I dared not accept. In such a highly organized home as the Lensteins', my peculiarity could not have been kept hidden forever. Besides, I had further reservations.

Lucie's love grew stronger by the day, and she drew ever closer to me. Was I permitted to betray the trust of these noble people who firmly believed that it was merely my good influence that chained the girl to me? No. I could not and did not want to repay their kindness so shabbily and thus refused their offer. At first, they did not want to accept my refusal. Finally, I had to promise to remain with them at least until the end of the semester.

Ties of friendly comradeship bound me to Lucie's brother, Fritz, a talented young painter. We spoke of everything that moved us, especially of social and moral questions. He offered, as a supplement to our conversations, to guide me through the narrow streets and alleyways where the poorest inhabitants of Hamburg lived in sordid conditions. I saw the areas at first by day, and then by night, too, as the life in those streets is most typical at night. We also passed through the streets where prostitutes are quartered. My companion graphically described the circumstances of these unfortunate human beings, who bear the yoke of personal exploitation and social ostracism.

Lucie declined to participate in our studies. The project seemed to her to be too unfeminine. But she was jealous of Fritz, to whom I devoted so much time.

At any rate, these fancy-free expeditions were a rather strange undertaking for a young lady. Herr Lenstein, who had meanwhile returned from his journey, thought so, too. His wife, however, hotly defended me. I was such an unusual individual that I could permit myself such a project. In this way, I could perhaps gather experience that would prove useful to all of womankind.

I soon stood on a comradely footing with Herr Lenstein, too. He occupied a position with the harbor authority. Under his guidance, I first made acquaintance with the large ships that carry emigrants to their new homes. He showed me the free port and gave me an opportunity to acquaint myself with the colorful activity in the customs offices, with their thousands of articles from all over the world. But most of all, it was the emigrants who interested me. I occupied myself much with them, struck up conversations, and gained many an insight into their personal circumstances and the economic conditions in their native countries. A sheer abyss of misery emerged before my eyes, so that I resolved to look more deeply into these questions; perhaps an appeal to public opinion would prove to be of use.

Herr Lenstein provided me with statistical material so that I could conduct scientific studies. The fact that my previous studies had often brought me into contact with Russians, Rumanians, and Galicians made this situation familiar to me. When I asked for material, it was most willingly given to me.

Among the emigrants were numerous interesting types. Big-boned Croatians; slender, delicate Polish ladies; melancholy, impoverished Jews who had been driven out of Russia; wild Rumanians in their national costume; and clumsy Ruthenians in their white furs: a lively picture and yet so monotonous in its gray misery. I became interested in the emigrants' native countries and thus read many German translations of Russian novels during this time, among others *King Lear of the Steppe* by Turgenev. It tells of an old man from whom everything has been taken, including his knife, and how he finally burns off his beard over the flame of a candle. My own heavy beard was making more difficulties for me year by year. I did not wish to shave, so as not to be betrayed by the black stubble, so I had been removing my hair with tweezers. That was very painful and only helped for a short time. Now I attempted to burn it off. That worked better and was a more radical solution.

I noticed that there were a great number of women and girls among the emigrants. I thought that this matter was of interest for women, too, and made use of the results of my studies in several essays in which I set down not only the facts but also looked into their causes. In doing so, I could hardly avoid shedding light on the political and social circumstances in the relevant countries. At this time, major debates on Poland were being conducted in the German Reichstag, and the turmoil in Hungary also attracted public attention. This contributed much to the fact that my articles received widespread attention. I signed them with a short form of my first name.

One day, through the offices of the editor, I received a letter from a major German-American newspaper, saying approximately the following: "We have read your articles and ask you to call on our representative in Germany. You write very lucidly about Poland and the Poland Question, which is very much of general interest at present, and especially interests Germans in America. Would you like to travel to Poland on our behalf and to Siebenbürgen, where the Germans are being oppressed? We ask you for your conditions, and above all request that you call on us."

At first we laughed heartily at their assumption that a man had written my articles, and strongly regretted that I would miss this great opportunity. Finally, I did in fact call on Mr. Webber, and introduced myself. At first, he was very disappointed to see a woman and asked for time to think it over. In the end, we reached an agreement, and I undertook to go on the journey under conditions that were very advantageous for me.

The doctors had prescribed a stay at a beach resort for Frau Lenstein. Lucie and I accompanied her to a quiet spa on the North Sea. Herr Lenstein came to visit every Sunday. We went for long walks, accompanied by Frau Lenstein, who quickly recovered in the bracing sea air.

On the last Sunday before my departure, we went for a walk and came to a small fishing village.

Over the village lay a strange uneasiness, which disconcertingly differed from the placid, peaceful Sunday atmosphere the people there usually paused to enjoy. We were told that the son of one of the guests at the spa had drowned while swimming. His father had offered a reward for the recovery of the corpse.

On the village street, groups of people stood around everywhere, discussing the tragic accident. In a dark doorway, an old fisherman was busily sorting the tools of his trade. When asked what he was looking for, he replied, in the northern German vernacular of the region, "Nothing but corpse hooks, my dears, nothing but corpse hooks. I want to catch myself a fine fish today!"

Utterly horrified, we listened to this coarse, insensitive remark. Lucie clung nervously to my arm and pressed my hand to her breast, which was heaving with passionate agitation. My heart, too, beat faster.

We had arrived in the village after a glorious walk along the sea, upon which the late afternoon sun was shining. It spread out before us, gleaming blue, and our conversation had been merry. Now our exuberant mood was replaced by a feeling of oppression about the tragic accident.

Some refreshment, partaken of at an inn, failed to lighten our mood. The strong drink, to which we were unaccustomed, only increased our agitation. Lucie's face twitched painfully. We felt uneasy, and, no longer able to bear being indoors, we stepped back outside. With our arms wrapped tightly around each other, we walked to the beach. It had grown dark, as dark as it can be only on a summer evening when the moon is shining and painting trembling circles on the deep green water. We walked along the soft sand of the dunes, toward the water. The tide was in. The waves came slowly closer, gobbling up the fine lines in the yellow sand as if with greedy lips. Lucie pressed close to me. I put my arm around her shoulder and lightly caressed her hair. It was quite silent on the beach. Now and again, when a boat drifted past or the dying sound of oars reached us from afar, the waves increased their murmur. Otherwise there was no sound, no life. Not a soul was on the beach. Before us lay the sea, whose waters glided by, singing peacefully. We remembered the dead man, and our bodies pressed closer together. He lay somewhere down below, stiff and cold. But life raced through our veins, wilder and fiercer than ever.

Lucie flung herself down onto the sand. I wanted to stretch out next to her, but she pressed me passionately to her, so that our bodies lay closely touching. And in a touchingly soft voice, she murmured again and again, "I am so fond of you, I long for you so!"

"I am fond of you, too, from the bottom of my heart, and I am here with you," I replied. "So how can you still long for me?"

"I don't know, but I feel a longing. I want to be very close to you. Do you know how? I am ashamed."

With hot, trembling lips, she kissed my hands.

Ecstatic passion took possession of me then, and I covered her mouth with burning kisses.

A ship passed by very close to the shore. We walked home, lost in dreamy thoughts. My hand lay around her waist, the rhythm of her steps gently rocking my body.

Anyone else in my position would have been overjoyed at being appointed to such a lucrative and honorable position immediately after university. But I never experienced a feeling of perfect happiness. I suffered more and more from the wild desires of my young, inflamed senses. I also suffered from the attention my beard received, in spite of all my efforts to remove the sprouting hairs. Compared with me, every young farmer's lad and every maid was to be envied. They clearly knew the essence of their being, whereas I, in spite of my advanced learning, was still left groping in the dark.

After a short stay with my mother, I began my journey, provided with letters of recommendation and sufficient funds. I had received instructions to spare no expense if there was an opportunity of seeing something of interest. Besides, travel is easy in the countries I visited, once one has grasped the proper way of dealing with the officials.

One day I had a certain distance to cover, slightly more than the distance between Berlin and Breslau. However, my ticket covered a journey only as far as the third or fourth stop from my point of departure, for I had originally intended to spend the night there. At the last minute, I had been warned about the hotels in that town, and so preferred to spend the night on the train rather than in an obscure, dirty, cheap hotel with unwanted tiny bedfellows.

I gave the conductor money for a ticket to R., my final destination, and asked him to wake me when we arrived there in the morning. Half an hour before our arrival, the conductor knocked. I asked for my ticket, but he laughed mischievously. "Come on, little mother, I'm not so stupid. I didn't buy a ticket with your money at all. I thought the inspectors were unlikely to come around at night, and anyway, why should the railway company earn the good money? I'll be damned! Let us earn it! You for cake, and I for *vodka*!"

And that is not an isolated example by any means.

The letters of recommendation smoothed my way into all circles of society. I received much hospitality, probably because people feared or hoped that I would mention them in my accounts of my travels.

The journey proved extremely instructive. I became acquainted with many interesting people, party leaders, industrialists, members of parliaments, and, above all, women's organizations in those countries.

My journal contains an episode from that period, which is typical of how I felt with regard to my belonging to one of the sexes. I always spoke of myself in the German masculine form. I always said, "I am a (male) student, a (male) reporter"; I never used the feminine form of these words.

This impulsive habit once caused a scene, which could easily have become dangerous for me. It was during a trip to a small Hungarian town on the edge of the Carpathian Mountains. My passport had been stolen, and I reported the theft in a police station.

"What is your occupation?" asked the officer.

"I am a newspaper correspondent [masculine form]."

"Nationality?"

"German [masculine form]."

"Oho," said the policeman, "you seem very suspicious to me! You look like a man, and speak like a man, and in the end you even say that you are a German using the masculine form, not a German in the feminine form of the word? That is very suspicious!"

The whole thing started to become unpleasant. Finally, a lady luckily recognized me, as she had seen my picture and a description of me in a women's magazine. Otherwise, the whole affair could have become very embarrassing for me.

I found that large parts of the population were destitute. One could hardly imagine a more tragic situation.

The female population in particular lives in abject poverty, and, as instructed, I focused on them. I cannot deny myself the opportunity of describing with an example the poverty of the above-mentioned women.

In a town that is well known for the export of agricultural produce, I found an employer for whom about thirty women were working.

Of the thirty girls, four or five had been to school, and the most educated had attended lessons for two years. The workers were between eleven and thirty years old. The working day was twelve hours, with an hour for lunch. The wages they earned were between twenty and fifty pfennigs, depending on age and skill, by the day that is, and not by the hour! By the way, only the forewoman received fifty pfennigs.

Educated women are usually strangers to the uneducated. There is bitter hatred between the rich and the poor.

I spoke at many women's associations in order to serve the cause of women's rights as far as possible. But the effect of my lectures was limited by the fact that they had to be translated.

The authorities were usually very accommodating. Only in one town did the mayor refuse to let me have the room in the town hall that was usually set aside for such lectures. What was the reason? He disliked the title of my lecture "Unemployment and Indecency." As a result, the stern patriarch of the town declared that he could not allow such an immoral lecture to be held in "his" hall and was only reassured after I had changed the title to suit him.

I achieved cult status. People asked for my autograph, and on some evenings I sold my signature a dozen times for a good cause.

I also carried on a lively trade in my hair. How far objective enthusiasm contributed to my popularity, and how far an unconscious sensuous attraction played a role, I naturally do not know. The wife of a parliamentarian once said to me, "When you speak, you exude a strange aura, such as I have never felt in another female speaker. I only feel something similar when my husband speaks."

Another lady said to me after a major public speech: "You really hypnotize us. It is as if you are emitting a strong current that forces us to listen to you with bated breath and to look at you. One just *has* to adore you."

In fact, women are much more easily enthused and moved by me than men, and I find it very easy to convince women of my point of view during lectures. I am often able to win them over to ideas that were far from their minds beforehand. This sometimes led to one-sided gestures of friendship that I could not return because of their large number.

Thus, it was by no means surprising that I was often invited to stay in private homes. At first, I strongly resisted this. But an experience, which I wish to relate here, soon cured me of this bashfulness.

I was to speak in a town of approximately twelve thousand inhabitants in northern Hungary. In the vicinity of this town, carpet weaving as a cottage industry is widespread, and the desire to learn more about the wages paid and the sale of the carpets brought me to Lomanosz, the center of this industry. At the same time, I had accepted an invitation to speak at a local women's association that devoted itself to "occupations for women." They had reserved a room for me at the best hotel and, at my request, had given it a cursory inspection for cleanliness.

At a late hour, after a very cozy evening, I was escorted to my inn, the Cour Royal. Frankly, a sense of horror overcame me at the mere sight of the outside of the building. At the door, the usual leave-takings took place. First the mayor's wife bade me farewell and, with a few kind words, pressed a package into my hand. I was just about to say that I did not accept payment for my lectures when she whispered softly, "Oh, please do accept it, it is merely a small token!" Thanking her, I slipped the package into my pocket and turned to the Madame President who, with an embarrassed smile, handed me a small bottle. In vain, I tried to refuse, because I never use perfume, but my protests were of no use, and it was the same with a third and fourth lady, so that finally I landed in my room with seven of these tokens of appreciation. I undressed, and as the air in the room was not particularly pleasant, I reached for what I took to be the bottle of perfume, silently thanking the friendly lady who had so kindly guessed my needs beforehand. But when I removed the paper, I did not find perfume but a flacon of insect powder. Surprised and amused, I opened the other small package, a box of "genuine Persian insect powder, unmatched in the extermination of insects of all kinds." "Oh, God, how quaint," I thought, dismayed, and opened number three: "Soriso-fon, the best thing for moths, fleas, flies, and other pests." Number four proved to be an atomizer for the delights in boxes one to three. Five and six were tinctures to be rubbed in, and thus protect from any bites, and number seven was the familiar powder again. Each token was accompanied by a card from the donor, wishing me a "good night"! "Yes, a good night," I thought, and sighed uneasily. After wasting a bottle of tincture and two of powder, I lay down. Around midnight, I awoke and reached with both hands for my face, which was burning unbearably. I could not stand the torment for long. I then got up and created horrible carnage.

Afterward, I lay down on the gray leather sofa, hoping to find peace there. An hour later, I awoke again. This time, my hands were badly swollen. I spent the rest of the night on a large oak table. The next morning, I left the Cour Royal very quickly. I had certainly lost all respect for it during the night.

This experience, and ones like it, caused me to avoid hotels altogether in small towns and to accept private hospitality instead. But this, too, had its drawbacks. People are very uninhibited in that country. In such cases, my hostess always wanted to talk to me as much as possible and sometimes arrived in my room when I was still lying in bed. Naturally, I was nervous during those visits, a fact that once attracted the attention of a lady. "Are you embarrassed in front of me? But that is utter nonsense, one woman in front of another! In spite of your position in public life, you are still so delightfully naive!"

Quite often I even had to share a room with my hostess when her husband was away on a journey. Once I had to share a bed with a young girl. The thought of this was at first quite terrible to me. The girl kissed me wildly, but no intimate relations ensued. She just felt the man in me. There is a knowledge of the body that is stronger than all logic.

My expression was quite masculine and attracted attention among women. Most women found me very appealing. Ties of genuine friendship bound me to some of them. But in spite of that, most of them remained inhibited by the strangeness of my nature. Generally, women are very uninhibited with their own kind; they undress freely and do not find the presence of others disturbing. In spite of the deep spiritual trust many women displayed toward me, such uninhibited behavior did not happen in my presence.

The fact that clothing influences the feelings and judgment of most people is shown by some newspaper reports about my lectures.

One paper writes: "Nora O. B. is an excellent speaker who combines masculine determination with genuine feminine charm."

A report in another newspaper in the winter of 1904 says: "Yesterday one had the opportunity to see a young and beautiful lady, sagacious, . . ."

Quite often, I was assured that someone was astounded and had not believed that one could combine my profession with so much genuine femininity.

Sometimes such reviews amused me. Mostly, though, they made me sad. I envied every man who was able, without being fettered by custom or constraint, to develop all his mental and physical faculties, while my path was blocked at every turn by the barrier of "that is not befitting."

The women's association in Starnovo invited me to give a lecture. The town is so small and insignificant that I hardly would have accepted if its unique character had not attracted me: Starnovo is one of the oldest settlements in the Ukraine.

The ladies from the committee of the association met me at the station. I said a few kind words to each of them, and then walked toward the town with the person who had invited me to luncheon. My beautiful, elegant, slender companion stood out advantageously from the other ladies of Starnovo. Her clothing was discreet and of fine quality, her voice melodious. She had a young face but, and one did not notice this at once, a veil of weariness hung over her eyes; in her gaze lay a deep longing.

It was a dull day in November, and the poorly paved roads stood deep in water. The bleak, dreary sight influenced my mood. I know not what confused me. An anxious feeling of expectation overcame me. From time to time, I furtively glanced at my companion's face and met her eyes, which gazed at me in amazement. The way to her house was not far. After dinner, I wanted to go to my hotel, but she told me that my luggage had been brought to her house, and I would now have to spend the night with her.

After some hesitation, I agreed. After the lecture, we returned home together. We then undressed, and conversed for a long time until we fell asleep. When I wished to continue my journey the next morning, Hanna Bernhardovna, I called her by her first name, as is customary in that country, and she called me Fräulein Nora, asked me so kindly to stay for a few more days that I agreed. It gave me pleasure to gaze upon this beautiful and appealing creature. I had watched her dressing and found only one word: a queen! It is unlikely that any other man has had the opportunity of seeing and comparing as many women as I have. I searched for a comparison and found only that word.

After breakfast I sat at a desk, making entries in my journal. I was unable to write, for my ears were filled with strange sounds, and my hands were unable to hold the pen. They longed to tousle that glorious blond hair, and my mouth longed for kisses. Then I heard the door being opened. When I looked up, I met the blue eyes of my hostess. She drew up a chair, put her arm around me, and looked at me. "You are so dear, I want to kiss you. May I?" Smiling, I held out my cheek, but although her lips barely touched me, I felt myself turn pale at this fleeting touch. We went over to the piano. In a soft alto, she sang lieder by Schumann, and I felt as though I had never understood the melodies as well as on that day.

We spoke of a wide variety of issues. She was wise, and because of her calm and assured manner, anyone who was not able to see beyond the surface might have thought her happy. But she was not. Our conversation turned to my mission, and I told her that I wished to spend some time in the capital of the neighboring province. I then learned that she had been born there.

My journals contain only few entries for those days. I grew very fond of Hanna Bernhardovna, and admired the harmony of her beauty. Her proud walk, her erect posture, her whole being matched her queenly appearance.

Taking leave was very difficult for me. From my compartment in the train, I looked back for as long as I could, and missed her for days. Then my work helped me forget.

A few days later, I arrived in N., the town where Hanna Bernhardovna had been born, and the place where I wished to continue my activities. When I went out one morning, I encountered Hanna Bernhardovna at a street corner. My heart beat faster when I espied her. I wanted to walk toward her and greet her, but while my whole heart longed to go to her, a strange heaviness lay upon my limbs. I could hardly move my feet forward. It was the same with her; a happy smile lit up her face when she saw me. Hand in hand we stood a while thus, lost in one another's gaze. We forgot the people around us. Only when some passersby looked at us in amazement did we remember the time and place. Hanna put her arm through mine, and pulled me away. The light in her eyes transformed the dull November day for me. Heavy and weak-willed, her hand lay on my arm. We walked along without paying attention to the way, and suddenly found ourselves in a remote field outside the town.

We gazed at one another in surprise and did not know how we had arrived there. Then we both laughed, carefree with joy.

We kissed again and again, and when her lips touched my mouth a wonderful feeling of sinking into an endless ocean overcame me.

I spent much time with Hanna during my sojourn. Either I visited her at her parents' home, or she came to my hotel. I was puzzled by the power she possessed to suddenly occupy all to my thoughts. Whenever I was working, her blond head appeared before my mind's eye. She, too, thought of me all day long. I walked about in a sweet dream, and feared awakening. What kind of miracle had happened to me?

Hanna came to my hotel early in the morning. I awaited her in tortured suspense. Every step I heard on the stairs caused my heart to beat faster. And when she actually arrived, I was incapable of speech, could only walk toward her, kiss her and bury my face deep in the fur that I slowly removed from her shoulders. We spoke little. When finally she was seated by my side on the sofa, we quietly held hands and felt the flow of feeling that carried our longing from heart to heart. From time to time we kissed, and then sat silent once more.

Every morning, the feverish longing began. To go to her. Everything else seemed irrelevant. Nothing of what we had once considered important mattered to us any longer. But as soon as we were together, the fear of parting weighed on us in spite of the joy we felt. Parting every evening was painful, and although the separation was short, we put off saying farewell again and again.

When I could no longer postpone my departure any longer, she accompanied me to the next town to which I went. We had a common acquaintance there who invited us both to stay with her. Thus, we were together from early morning to late in the evening. And still we found even those days too short. We always had more to say to one another while we sat hand in hand, looking into one another's eyes, it was torture, ecstasy, joie de vivre, and yet deathly fear. An overpowering natural force led us irresistibly to each other and united us forever. All duty paled, all the people who entered our lives then darted past like shadows.

Worries and doubts tortured me again and again. What was I really? A man? Oh, God, no. That would have been indescribable joy. But miracles no longer happen nowadays. I knew nothing anymore. My whole life seemed like a powerful illusion that covered up the truth. Everyone considered me to be a woman; even my dear friend called me Nora. How could I ever have thought I was a man? I was an abnormally formed girl, that was all. But this feeling? I did not know; neither of us did. Could this joyous, compelling power be a vice? Could being intoxicated with the purest of joys, the most beautiful thing in life be a vice? Deep fountains within us gushed forth. Together we learned to understand and enjoy the arts. Her listening ear drank in the beauty of the verses I read to her, and she sang only for me: Schumann and Mendelssohn and the sweet, dusky folk melodies of the Ukraine. Miraculously, I quickly learned to speak and understand her language.

What was this feeling that irresistibly bound us to each other? Deep love. I know not whether this love inspired our senses or whether it made our souls more receptive, but it spun its threads between us and wove our destinies together. We were one. Every fiber of our beings trembled together, every emotion was felt in both our hearts at one and the same time.

One morning, I wanted to leave for a meeting at eight o'clock without having seen Hanna. I dressed in a dark mood, tore open the window, and looked out. The biting November wind whistled around my head and cooled my burning temples. Apathetically, I went to the conference and only half-listened to the questions that were on the agenda, thinking only of the hour when I would see Hanna once more.

Those few days in the peaceful provincial town were some of the happiest in my life.

One day, we went for a walk with a lady whom we knew slightly. Hanna walked ahead on the narrow path. She was wrapped in fine gray furs. Her blond hair, which could be seen underneath her upturned hat, shone against the dark gray of her collar. My gaze was fixed on her, and only with difficulty could I follow the chatter of my acquaintance. My soul was with Hanna, and I could speak of nothing but her. I began to tell my acquaintance about my dear friend, my friend whom I had known only for two weeks! I spoke to this acquaintance of our friendship and had the feeling that it had existed for many years. I was completely in the throes of this deception and could not, in my dream-like state, distinguish illusion from truth. And in the twilight of the winter's evening that wrapped itself around us, the woman walked before me who carried my soul within her.

We spent nine days in that town. In order to have an excuse for this long sojourn, I held several lectures. When Hanna was present, I had eyes only for her. Otherwise, I had nothing to do with anyone, for I wanted to rest and conserve my strength as far as possible. As an exception, in Hanna's presence, I did twice receive a gentleman who had introduced himself to us after a lecture. He was a young lawyer who wished to ask me abut a point in German publishing law. He seemed shy and in low spirits.

When we departed, he came to the station with a large bouquet of flowers. As I was talking to some ladies from the women's association, he turned to Hanna and gave her the roses to give to me.

Once again, we spent three days in the capital. A letter had arrived from my editorial department, requesting that I call on our European representative as soon as possible in order to negotiate a new contract with him. Thus, our parting drew near, and an unspeakably sad atmosphere lay over us.

One afternoon, I received a registered express letter. Hanna read the address and handed it to me. It was from the lawyer who had presented the fragrant greetings at the station. I opened the letter with a combination of curiosity and annoyance at the intrusion.

"This must be a misunderstanding, dear Hanna," I said to my friend, "for I think this letter contains a declaration of love. The man must mean you, and must have confused our names." Hanna read the letter. "No, it is for you," she decided.

I have kept the letter, which is written in the somewhat clumsy German of a foreigner. It reads:

My dear Madam,

On the one hand, it is the all-too-great agitation in which I now find myself that prompts me to communicate to you in writing, a matter that I would like to discuss with you personally, but on the other I am doing so because I wish the matter to which my letter pertains to lead to a serious decision, not hastily made . . .

My dear Madam! As great an effort as I am making to express myself concisely and clearly, what I have written remains only a weak and unclear expression of what I think, a barely noticeable reflection of the feelings that overcome me, Madam! I love you!

I barely spoke to you twice, and saw you but once or twice, but that was enough to make such an impression on me that I must honestly admit: I love you . . .

Do not consider this the prank of a rash youth, do not view it as something that dishonors you, for it is the purest and most powerful feeling that can grow in a man's breast, and if you demand proof, then my life is at your disposal, I lay it at your feet.

Although I neglected to tell you all this when you left our town, I still feel and know all too well that things cannot go on this way. I must evoke an answer now, be it as bad for me as it may, for my life in this terrible uncertainty has become more of a burden than death, which remains open to me in the worst of cases. . . .

Thus I beseech you:

Will you shorten the torment of uncertainty for one who loves and admires you fiercely, and communicate to him, whether he may cherish a tiny, but for him so auspicious, hope to one day see this love returned by his beloved?

I am only too well aware of the fact that I am placing in your hands a verdict over life and death, but I am doing so, as I can no longer bear the agonizing doubt.

That is what I wished to tell you; now discharge your judgmental duty . . .

The letter dismayed me, but we could not resist the tragicomic impression this declaration of love made on us.

"Poor devil," said Hanna and brought me my writing materials. The impetuous lover received an answer to his unsuccessful declaration of love that same day. I answered him that his letter had not offended me, but rather greatly surprised me. I could only beg of him to forget what he had written; he should devote himself to the great challenges of our civilization, and then we would meet in our loyalty to the people.

I shall follow up here with an excerpt from his answer:

"I have understood from it, your firm decision, which makes you seem even more lofty and sublime. Still, I abandon myself to the hope that one day, when you have tired of your great and magnanimous task, you may feel the need of the help and support of a strong man's arm. Then perhaps the hour of my good fortune may arrive."

I found it oddly moving that I was able to inspire such deep love in a man, and it confused me even more. I also felt sorry for the poor man. Hanna, too, felt sorry for him; we both knew how unhappy hopeless love can make one. How odd that this proposal, which, by the way, was not the only proposal of marriage I received, should come now, of all times.

January had arrived. It could no longer be postponed. Hanna had to return to Starnovo, I to Berlin. The day of our parting arrived, and unhappy months followed, hours of despair, which we endured only in the hope of meeting again, after which we would never again have to part, for that would be harder to bear than death.

In Berlin, I met with the representative of my newspaper. He commissioned me to travel to Norway in the winter. In spring, I was to tour Turkey to study the life and social conditions of women there.

The winter in Norway seemed well-nigh endless. I saw the beauty of the Nordic mountains but could not savor it. It was as though a part of me was with Hanna and as if my feelings were paralyzed because she was not with me. My heart was restless, dissatisfied, and full of worries. Although we wrote each other daily, the letters were but poor consolation for months of separation. We considered our future prospects. What was to become of us? There was no way out, and no salvation, so we decided to die.

During my studies in Berlin, I had met a young doctor who was devoted to me. When I returned from Norway in the spring, I visited him and asked him for poison. He refused to grant my wish until I told him it was for the purpose of putting an end to my suffering and the suffering of a dear friend, which had been caused by our longing for each other. We wished to be joined forever. As life was unable to grant us that joy, we wished to go to our deaths together. After some hesitation, he gave me morphine.

It was a late afternoon in March when I visited him in his laboratory. We sat at his desk until it grew dark. Then he accompanied me through the fresh spring air of Tiergarten Park to my hotel. Speaking calmly of the last things to be done, we walked along. I was lost in deep thought, not paying attention to the direction in which we were going, and thus hardly noticed that we were walking along a very lonely path. My companion spoke to me persuasively. He warned me against this step, and described the consequences to me.

"Look, my dear friend," he said, and his voice became ever more persuasive, "the world has so much more to offer! You are still young and have a great future before you. And you do not yet know the sweetest thing in life. If you really wish to die, then before you do, savor the rest of your days. Love, and enjoy yourself!"

The path was lonely. I looked around me. His manner, which departed from his usual calm, disconcerted me. He spoke forcefully to me in a hoarse voice. Suddenly, he tried to draw near and put his arms around my waist. At that moment, I found my strength once again. With a gesture of loathing and rage, I straightened up and slapped his face.

The next minute, he rushed off without saying a word. My slap had lost me a friend.

The days remaining to me in Berlin were full of torment and impatience. I wrote endless letters to Hanna, and we exchanged telegrams almost every day, but still our separation weighed unbearably on us. Neither work nor amusement could distract me from my yearning, which made me impervious to the bustle and appeal of the big city.

One day when I jumped from the tram, I injured my foot. I was taken to my rooms, and a doctor was summoned. I was stunned by my mishap, which would force me to postpone our reunion once more. This new sorrow almost overwhelmed me. I missed Hanna everywhere. I was forced to hide our secret in the deepest depths of my heart, but I felt the need to tell someone of our ill-fated, hopeless love. The day before, I had gone hesitantly to a Catholic church to confess, to empty my heart to one of the priests who did not know me and whom I would never see again. But when I had stood for a while in the church, which smelled heavily of incense, I found that I lacked the necessary courage, and left with a heavy heart.

While lying in bed, waiting for the doctor, I was thinking of all this. When he finally arrived, he found me in tears. He was surprised at the severe pain I seemed to be suffering, judging from the deep sobs that wracked my body in spite of my efforts to control myself. He asked whether the pain was so great, or whether I had other troubles. My deep sorrow moved him. He drew up a chair, stroked my hair, and said in a kind, fatherly tone of voice, "Don't cry, dear child. There are few things in this world which are worth so many tears. Wouldn't you like to unburden your heart to me? Perhaps you will feel relieved afterward!"

I stared at him. Could I trust this man? His calm, finely featured face, which was turned toward me in friendly sympathy, and his entire manner gave me confidence in him. I recalled my desire to confess. A doctor was bound to silence by his professional duty, and I had to speak. I no longer had the strength to bear my suffering in silence. So I took his hands and told him what gave us such joy and was, at the same time, so ill-fated and made us so unhappy. His face remained calm and friendly. Then he asked me a number of questions. I told him the story of my childhood, the secret of my body, and spoke to him of the countless sorrows and humiliations of bygone days. A heavy burden was gradually lifted from my soul as I at last spoke openly of what had depressed me for so long.

The doctor listened in silence and then said I would have to allow him to examine me thoroughly. When he finished, he spoke to me encouragingly. There was no reason to be sad. My love for my lady friend was no vice, and, by the way, as far as love was concerned, there was no vice, perhaps only in sensuousness, it was a natural feeling. "If you wish to be close to your friend and you can secure a future for her, then go ahead and marry her! You are as much a man as I am!" Only a minor operation, which he explained to me, was needed. The doctor in Bergheim who had examined me at birth was an ass. Moreover, my body seemed to have developed in a decidedly masculine way only during the last few years. I should take courage; the authorities could not deny permission for my transformation, and then I could marry my lady friend with a clear conscience.

It was as though dark veils had been torn from my eyes. The doctor was right. Physically, I was a man. And I had often been told that I had the spirit of a man.

A frenzy of joy and delight overcame me. I no longer heard what the kind old gentleman was saying. I lay there with my eyes shut, dreaming. For years, I had been unable to find the words for prayer; now I was overcome by an ecstatic, fervent thankfulness to God. I forgot where I was, saw Hanna's face, radiant with joy.

The doctor stood beside me and, with a friendly nod, shook my hand.

I lay still for many hours. The new state of affairs was so overwhelming that I could not yet seriously grasp it. Now a bright light lay on our dark path.

For three days, I lay in a fever. The doctor came every day, and he had retained the services of a discreet and reliable nurse. I know nothing of my feverish dreams. I only remember that I lived in regions of boundless bliss.

I regained consciousness only on the third day. The severe fever had weakened me so much that I was able to recover my strength only slowly. The delight of the reawakening of my strength was mixed with joyful thoughts of a happy future.

I had not actually wanted to write Hanna of the happy turn in our destiny, partly because I feared the letter might be lost and partly because I did not know how she would bear the joyous missive. In the end, however, I hinted at the content of my discussion with the doctor. Joyfully, she wrote back to me. Yes, at last, this was the path to happiness. I should have the change done, and then she would free herself for me. First, though, we must see one another once more.

A new tone entered our letters. They became more intimate and at the same time more confident.

At last, the business that kept me in Germany was completed. I received the new commission to report on the life of women in Turkey.

One day in early spring, I began my journey. Of course, I went first to Starnovo, without telling Hanna beforehand of my arrival. After two long torturous days of travel, at last I saw the Carpathian Mountains appear in the distance. Soon I began passing familiar places. There, on that mountain, was a glade in which we had rested during a walk, and that gray country road led directly to the station. Then the conductor pulled open the door: "In five minutes, we will be arriving in Starnovo. One minute stopover!" There on the platform she stood, pale with excitement, anxious with expectation. I leaped out before the train had even stopped. We were at a loss for words and held hands in dumb silence, gazing into each other's eyes. The carriage that was to take us to her home was too slow for us, so we got out and walked. People on the streets stared after us. They had probably seldom seen such a rapturous pair.

But the joy we were able to savor in this home that belonged to another was actually only imperfect. On the morning after my arrival, we went for a walk. We walked arm in arm, and the beat of her heart echoed in mine. Silently, we walked through the streets of the town. At the old city gate, Hanna let go of my arm and looked at me questioningly. We sat down on a fallen log by the side of the road, and I spoke to her of my plans. One thing was for sure: I now wanted to break with my life as a woman and become a man at last. I wanted to take up an occupation of some kind that would enable me to earn a living.

Would she then allow me to come and fetch her? But it would take a long time before I would be able to surround her with the luxury to which she was accustomed; would she be willing to live with me under more modest circumstances? Then I could soon fetch her.

She looked at me proudly and trustingly. "You foolish darling," she laughed joyously, "will I be coming to your tables and chairs, or to you? What need have I of jewels and elegant clothing, if I am with you?" She began to imagine our future life, how she would manage our modest household, and how she would welcome me home when I returned in the evening from work.

First she would have to be free, make any sacrifice necessary to dissolve her marriage. Although the ties she must tear asunder were but superficial, she foresaw fierce battles.

I must not have my change done before her marriage was dissolved;

otherwise, they would probably prevent our union or make it more difficult.

In order to be discreetly near her, I should accept the commission to travel to Turkey.

I was unhappy not to be able to stand by her during the difficult days she had to struggle through. Would she remain strong? She had to fight everyone who had been foremost in her heart, for I now filled that place and was to do so forever after. Soon afterward, I took my departure. Hanna accompanied me to the station. On the way, we discussed our plans once more. Firmly determined, we parted after a heartfelt and painful leave-taking.

Hanna had much to endure. She bore it with trusting yearning for mutual happiness.

Meanwhile, I toured Turkey. I spent my days, which were sad and joyless, with longing in my heart. The few letters I received from her were the highlights of this bleak period.

Slowly, without my contributing to the process, her marriage was dissolved. For the time being, Hanna returned to her parents' home.

Thus, the summer of the new year approached. I wrote to my employer, the publisher of my newspaper, that, for reasons of health, I was unfortunately forced to withdraw from my position as a traveling correspondent. Then I returned to Germany, where the difficult task of acquainting my mother and siblings with my plans lay before me. Although I was of age and did not need her consent, I wished for peace and wanted to avoid causing my mother pain if at all possible. For the love for my lady friend had awakened my feelings for my family.

My old mother received the news more calmly than I had expected. "Do whatever you think best," she said. "But spare your siblings, and avoid causing unnecessary sensationalism and gossip!" Then, for the first time, we spoke openly of my life. My mother told me of my birth, of my father's resistance to medical help, and how very worried she had been about me, especially recently.

I had not dared to hope that she would understand me so readily.

During this period, shortly before the final decision, I still had to overcome many inner struggles. I considered the enormity of the step. Would I become accustomed to this new life? Would Hanna grow accustomed to the altered circumstances? And would I be able to provide her with an adequate livelihood?

But all those considerations disappeared at the blissful thought of a future at Hanna's side.

I found the idea of consulting a lawyer very embarrassing. After all, I still dressed in women's clothing and thought of the impression my strange words would surely make. Thus, I put off the first step from one day to the next. At last I finally screwed up my courage and went to see a lawyer, Dr. Gronemann (Berlin), who had once been recommended to me in another case.

We discussed the legal aspects of the matter and decided that it was necessary to obtain scientific certificates from renowned medical authorities, which were needed to justify my petition.

With copies of these certificates, I applied to the Minister of the Interior, who replied that he was not the proper addressee. Although my lawyer had immediately pointed out the futility of this step, I still had hoped to spare myself going through all the official channels, as my case was so unusual. My lawyer then sent the petition to the proper place. The senior civil servants responsible proved to be very obliging. At the end of December 1906, after lengthy correspondence, and after I had been personally interviewed repeatedly, we received the news that my petition had been granted.

I had already begun to change my outward appearance before official permission had been granted. As a first step, my hair had to be cut. When I had this done, I was still wearing women's clothing. The barber thought it was a sin to sacrifice such beautiful hair to a whim.

After my hair had been cut, the shape of my head was more visible; I was told that the masculinity of my expression now came into its own, and I thus looked quite odd in women's clothing. Some days later, I had myself measured for my first frock coat.

The first time I walked across the road in men's clothing, I felt such a great sense of uneasiness that I would have liked to turn back. Men's clothing is quite a bit lighter than ladies'; the wind had free access to my body, and, at first, it seemed improper to be going out in trousers without skirts on top. I imagined that everyone on the street was staring at me. This insecure feeling lasted for several days, until at last I grew accustomed to it. Another thing, however, to which I grew accustomed only with great difficulty, was greeting people. I repeatedly forgot to raise my hat, and nodded like a lady. Once when I asked directions of a gentleman in the street, his answer was so unfriendly that it surprised me, until it occurred to me that I had forgotten to raise my hat.

Altogether, social niceties caused me many a difficulty at first. For example, I had to greet the older gentlemen among my acquaintances before they greeted me now, which I regularly forgot to do, and had to be on my guard when conversing with ladies not to touch on subjects that a gentleman does not usually discuss with them. So as not to offend anyone, I was at first very taciturn; but I soon returned to my original uninhibited manner.

At this time, I first had myself photographed again and sent Hanna my picture. In general, people were of the opinion that I had changed for the better. She thought so, too, and I was very pleased that she did.

A gentleman whom I had known for years before my change had to be told of my secret. Later, he assured me that I seemed more familiar to him in the first half hour of our new acquaintance than I had during all the years before.

Recently, I made my first long journey wearing men's clothing. Whereas formerly I had always spent the night in the ladies' compartment, I was now forced to make do with the non-smokers' compartment. It was a strange feeling to spend the entire night together with so many men at such close quarters for the first time. So it seems that education and habit are able to produce strong inhibitions.

My body, which was no longer constricted by bodices and other tight articles of clothing, developed freely and became stronger. I now do gymnastics and other kinds of exercise to compensate for the forced prevention of a healthy development. These efforts have been rewarded by success. I have become stronger and broader, my posture is freer, and physically nothing is likely to remain of my girlhood years other than a slight furrow left behind from tight lacing.

Sorrow and grief had made me old; now I look happy and young—alas, far too young.

The greater freedom that I now enjoy has not really changed my outlook, because my attitudes and opinions were always masculine. Some new aspects have, however, been revealed to me.

These small freedoms are extremely pleasant. I can return home late at night without having to fear that every stupid lad may molest me; I am now at liberty to smoke in the street undisturbed and enjoy all the other little privileges that the lords of creation have reserved for themselves.

Some girlish tenderness of feeling remains to me. I do not enjoy listening to obscene stories and humorous magazines, and pictures "for gentlemen only" nauseate me.

Seldom have so many women unveiled their souls to a man as have to me. I feel deep sympathy and brotherly love for all women.

We met again, Hanna and I. My transformation did nothing to change the feeling of joy that flows through us as soon as we see each other. We feel an overpowering sense of belonging together and have decided to unite forever as soon as possible.

First I must look for an occupation that will enable me to set up house. That is not easy, for it must be an occupation that suits all aspects of my abilities and needs. As Nora O. Body, I doubtlessly would have found one more easily. What is considered the epitome of education for a woman may be called ignorance in a man, and conversely, all the knowledge a man has may be worthless, because our old-fashioned order values the intellectual achievements of men and women so differently. Certainly, the differences will always remain, but it is high time people stopped evaluating a person's concrete and abstract knowledge according to his or her sex.

All my hard-gained knowledge has proved difficult to apply. Although there are positions in which I could have put it to use, as a secretary at a newspaper or in a bank or a charitable organization, this path is closed to me, for I have no certificates or testimonials. They have all been issued to Nora O. Body and are almost useless to the young Norbert. I am barred from applying for any position that requires that one present one's certificates of birth and baptism, as my papers all contain the corrective addition. I also lack the certificate of higher learning that is so often required, and when asked where I received my education, my answer, "at a girls' lyceum," will certainly produce more consternation than satisfaction.

But in spite of all the obstacles that are still in my path today, I look to the future with optimism. I am certain that I will be able to earn a living for us by my work.

All these difficulties arose from the fact that I was mistakenly raised as a girl. I think that today, when the frontiers between the occupations for men and women are no longer as strict, it would be better to register and raise children who are at first of indeterminate sex as boys, because they could get ahead better later on. For those who later turn out to belong to the female sex, the broader education they receive as boys could only be useful when choosing an occupation.

It is true that strong characters always find their way, but why build up obstacles when smoother paths lead to the goal?

At the end of my book, I should like to say a word to all mothers. All the pain and confusion that I suffered and that made my life bitter came from a false sense of shame that seeks to veil all things sexual as being unclean.

But they only become unclean, yea mothers, because strangers and not you yourselves divulge the deep mysteries of nature to your children. Have no qualms about appealing to your children's healthy instincts with reasonable words; you will do more for them that way than allowing them to grow up with false half-truths. A girl who goes through life with a sense of knowledge will be far more easily capable of protecting herself spiritually and physically against filth than one who is kept half blind by an unwise mother who is foolishly proud of her children's ignorance.

If you lack the courage to speak openly to your children, see to it that it becomes the duty of schools to do so. Think of the dark hours and confusion that you once met with in your own youth.

How much suffering and how many battles would I have been spared if, either at home or at school, one single person had spoken earnestly and honestly to me about my sex! My youth would not have been so dark and devoid of joy.

Honest knowledge never drags one down, but rather liberates and elevates one! Where is the mother who does not wish to see her child pure and free? Therefore, let us show our children the paths that lead to purity and freedom!

With joyous eyes, I look to the future that lies before me like an endless landscape, filled with sunlight.

May life around us rage and thunder, I shall at last enter the battle of life as a person with equal rights, a strong will, and a glad heart.

This book tells a true story, the story of a pitiful life that had to pass through much confusion before the lonely wanderer found the right path. I did not want to write this book, but others convinced me that I owed it to mankind as a contribution to modern psychology and that I should write it in the interest of science and truth.

Epilogue

DR. MED. MAGNUS HIRSCHFELD

The memoir published here is a substantial and valuable addition to the scientific literature on cases of erroneous sex determination. For the first time, an intelligent person gives an exhaustive account of the deeply tragic results of an error for which we should make our weak human understanding responsible, rather than nature, which is so often wrongly blamed. Therefore, this autobiography may claim general attention far beyond the world of medicine or law, in more than one respect.

We see here how far-reaching conflicts may occur already in the souls of children, certainly an instructive example for our times in which we, unfortunately, have far too many occasions to read of suicides committed by schoolchildren and other tragedies involving children. For far too long, adults have underestimated not only the importance of childhood for life, but also of children and their significance as human beings.

We further see an absolutely classical example of the struggle between a congenital disposition and external influences, between the inherited and the acquired. We observe how, with elemental force, certain inner impulses break through barriers that education and environment have erected, and how in spite of everything, in the end it is the spirit that molds life.

The following holds true in the field of sexuality.

The sex of a person lies more in his mind than in his body, or to express myself in more medical terms, it lies more in the brain than in the genitals.

How reasonable were the regulations of the Frederican epoch, which were valid here until the year 1900, and which stipulated that all persons of doubtful sex shall, at the age of eighteen, decide *themselves* "to which sex they wish to belong." How incomprehensible in comparison is the fact that these and similar regulations have been entirely left out of today's civil code, as justified as its existence is.

A strange coincidence ordained that a few years after this corruption of the law, the exact and scientific research on hermaphroditism in human beings began, research that proved beyond a doubt that the above-mentioned is, with relation to every sexual characteristic, infinitely more widespread than previously thought. We now know that cases like the one described here are only extreme forms of intermediate sexual stages which, to a lesser extent, occur in a great variety of physical and mental forms. Indeed, it even seems questionable whether the modern view is correct, a view that sees in these deviations from the norm outright dysfunctions and deformities, or whether there is not more to be said for the view held in antiquity, which regarded them merely as curious varieties and special individuals within the human race. It is well known that in the art of antiquity, both in its spoken and visual forms, the hermaphrodite is one of the most popular figures.

It would be getting too far away from the issue to go into great detail on the questions that present themselves here. I will confine myself to making a number of practical suggestions, based on the case described here, similar to those that I made during a lecture to the Society for Social Medicine, Hygiene and Medical Statistics [Gesellschaft für soziale Medizin, Hygiene und Medizinalstatistik].

First, when there is doubt as to the sex of a newborn child and a doctor who is consulted (and midwives should be obliged by law to

see to it that this does indeed happen in such cases) is unable to remove the doubt, the only thing that seems to be scientifically justified
is to register the child as being of "indeterminate sex." Should the relatives hesitate to register the child in such a manner because of exist-
ing prejudices, in any case, it is better in principle to register the child
as a male and to raise it accordingly. This holds true for the following
reasons: for one thing, it seems as if, in the majority of cases that have
become known so far, the sex that is latent until puberty afterward
develops in a male direction. From an economic point of view, when
there has been an erroneous diagnosis, it is easier for a man to continue his life as a woman than for a person who has been raised as a
woman to continue life as a man.

Above all, a less prejudiced and clearer judgment of these people
must be a goal, too. For they are completely equal human beings from
a mental, ethical, and social point of view, and thus it is necessary that
instead of the disparagement, secret horror, and ridicule that they
formerly met with, there should be a more just, scientific, and humane
attitude.

The more we learn of transition between the sexes, the more we learn
of the usefulness for man and woman of granting the greatest possible freedom to the play of forces. In this, the old quarrel whether the
one sex is superior or inferior to the other is entirely futile. Both are
equally valuable and equally necessary; both have their good and less
good characteristics. The self-regulation of nature provides the best
guarantee for the well-being of the individual as well as of the whole.
At least, it is far more reliable than artificial rules and prohibitions
imposed by human beings.

The ancient demand of freedom, equal rights for all, has its roots
far more in the differences between people than in their sameness. In
order for every individual to develop freely and beautifully, everyone
must be given the same opportunities.

Charlottenburg, April 10, 1907

Afterword

In Search of Karl Baer

HERMANN SIMON

An observant person walking through Section III D of the largest Jewish cemetery in Europe, in Berlin Weissensee, will notice a conspicuous gravestone. Markers such as the large sandstone one in row fifteen, lying down rather than standing upright, are relatively unusual. There is no word or abbreviation in Hebrew on the stone; its three-line inscription provides only the following meager information:

Hanna Baer
6. 5. 1880
9. 3. 1909

The person buried here is Beile Baer née Heilpern, called "Hanna," and born on May 6, 1880, in Czernovitz (Bukovina). She died, not quite twenty-nine years old, on March 9, 1909, at 5:30 P.M. in Rixdorf, which at that time lay on the outskirts of Berlin. Today the area is called Neukölln and has long since become part of the city proper. She was buried here on March 14 at 2 P.M. The cemetery records from which we have taken this information reveal the fact that the cause of death was pneumonia.

Heinrich Heine once wrote: "For every single man is a world which is born and which dies with him; beneath every grave-stone lies a world's history."[1]

1. Heinrich Heine, *Pictures of Travel* (Leipzig: Voigt & Günther, 1857), p. 292.

This is true here, though it is not so much the short life of Beile Baer that is of interest to us. Rather, it is her second husband, Karl, whom she married on October 10, 1907, in Vienna in the synagogue on Müllnergasse[2] who commands our attention. Beile enters the story primarily because she was of the utmost importance for Karl's self-discovery. Indeed, as we shall soon see, he owed to her his very existence as a man. In his autobiography he wrote, "I . . . wish to speak here of the love of this woman who cleared the thorns from my path and transformed my life which had been nothing but dark torment into a joyous blessing." But who was this man who for most of his life called himself Karl M. Baer?

I am firmly convinced that we historians have a great friend in coincidence, for it must be put down to coincidence that in 1973, my mother, Marie Simon, obliged her family with the following story.

Herr and Frau Baer, Karl M. and Elza, were acquaintances of my parents. As a child, I was pleased when the Baers visited us or when we went to see them, because the conversation was always lively and stimulating. Mr. Baer was witty and scintillating.

When I asked why Frau Baer's given name was pronounced "Elsa" but spelled "Elza," I was told that the spelling was according to Polish orthography; Frau Baer, a Jewish Pole, had studied German in her native country. There was something peculiar about her husband's given name, too: it was Karl M., and his middle name was never written out. Whenever he was mentioned, it was as Karl M. Baer.

One day when the postman delivered a postcard with holiday greetings from Karl M. Baer, I was asked to show it to my aunt, Margarete Eger, because the greetings were also meant for her. I was seized by curiosity. I wanted to know what the "M" stood for, probably for an unusual, peculiar-sounding name? So

2. Certificate issued by the Israelitischen Kultusgemeinde, Vienna 70/IX/ 1907.

I asked my aunt. She fell silent and stood rooted to the spot like a pillar of salt. Only later did I understand her strange behavior. She was confronted with a conflict of duties. On the one hand, one must tell the truth, nothing but the truth; on the other, necessary discretion must be observed under all circumstances. So I repeated my question, until finally, she solemnly told me that the "M" stands for Martha and I was not to ask any further questions.

At that time, I was about ten or twelve years old, I found what I had been told peculiar, because men are not called Martha. As this scanty information had not satisfied my curiosity but only intensified it considerably, I turned to my father and asked him why Karl Baer also had the female name Martha. He told me that Baer had grown up as a girl and had written his autobiography under the pseudonym N. O. Body. It was called *Aus eines Mannes Mädchenjahren* (*Memoirs of a Man's Maiden Years*). I have remembered this information to this day but never wanted to read the book. In order to learn new details, I very cleverly consulted my father and my aunt alternately, always presenting fresh bits of information that I had just coaxed out of one or the other. Because of my accumulated knowledge, I soon became an initiate, and discretion was no longer necessary.

Now Margarete had no qualms about telling me what she remembered about Karl/Martha. Thus, for the first time, I heard a coherent story.

During the first decade of the twentieth century, my aunt belonged to a circle of young Jewish people with intellectual interests who discussed literary and scientific subjects. They also helped the destitute survivors of the Russian pogroms. A certain Fräulein Martha Baer was also a member of this circle, and my aunt Margarete had become friendly with her. Martha was a typical intellectual, remarkably astute and a leading thinker. She had a flat chest, hair on her face, and a distinctly male voice. Altogether she seemed very much like a man. This young woman smoked thick cigars, drank copious amounts of beer in huge swigs, and, in general, her unconventional manner attracted attention. My aunt went on to say that one day, Fräulein Baer bade farewell to her circle of friends because she was moving to another city; she had found a new professional challenge, a meaningful task. After some time, a young man named Karl Baer joined the group. He was the spitting image of

Martha, except he wore men's clothing. The most noticeable difference was a new hair style; instead of being pinned up in a braid, the hair was now cut short. All the members of the circle were exemplary in their tact and discipline, and did not hint that they realized that Martha and Karl were one and the same person.

My father had not been acquainted with Martha Baer but had come into contact with the young Karl, most likely through his Zionist work—at any rate, in a different context from that of my aunt. Independently, I asked them both the obvious question—why Herr Baer had been raised as a girl—and received the same information from both. Baer had been born in Eastern Europe, the son of devout Jewish parents who had registered him as a girl in order to prevent him from being conscripted into the army and being forced to break the Jewish ritual laws. Living in Germany as a person of German culture, with a highly developed sense of right and wrong, he had become ashamed of the legal incorrectness of what his parents had done, and had sorted out the matter. In order to cover up the embarrassment in his book, in which he had changed the facts, anyway, and in order to preserve his anonymity, he had pretended that certain outer deformities of the genitals had led to his true gender being misinterpreted.

By the time my mother became acquainted with Karl M. Baer—and I know from my grandfather's diaries that the two families met often, Baer was the director of the B'nai B'rith lodges in Berlin, U.O.B.B.[3] He had begun to work for them on December 1, 1920, and was living in the building that belonged to the lodges on Kleiststrasse 11 in the elegant western part of Berlin.

For a long time, I believed the story just as my mother told it, accepting as fact that Karl Baer had been registered and brought up as a girl

3. B'nai B'rith is the largest and oldest Jewish fraternal organization. It was founded in New York in 1843 by German Jews "for the purpose of instilling the principles of morality among the followers of the Jewish faith . . . and of inculcating charity, benevolence, and brotherly love as the highest virtues." *The Jewish Encyclopedia* (New York, 1916), 3:275.

so that he might avoid military service. During certain periods, this was not unusual.[4] If, as my grandfather and great aunt had claimed, he was born in Eastern Europe, it was the book's account that his gender had been misinterpreted at birth that was pure invention. But I now know that it is his Eastern European birth that is fictitious. About his gender indeterminacy and misidentification, he was telling the truth.

Unlike my mother, I was interested in the *Memoirs of a Man's Maiden Years.* I got hold of a copy, devoured it, and was possessed by the idea of clarifying the story and writing the history of Baer's life. I cannot describe here in full the paths I have followed over the course of more than three decades in pursuit of the facts. As far as the difficulties are concerned, suffice it to say that in reconstructing his life, the most challenging thing was to prove that Martha and Karl Baer were, in fact, the same person.

In order to do this, I first had to track down all the different Carl and Karl Baers listed in the pages of the "Berliner Adressbuch" (Book of Berlin Addresses) and ascertain who was identical to whom. The

4. In czarist Russia, under Nicholas I (1825–55), Jews had to serve in the army for twenty-five years, which meant that the life of those involved was not only interrupted but often ruined. Children were taken away from their parents or caught in the streets and then disappeared forever. Although military service began at the age of eighteen, Jewish boys as young as eight were enrolled by force in special preparatory institutions. The purpose was to alienate them from their families, Russify them, and baptize them. Even after this rigorous practice was discontinued in 1856, military service was fraught with moral conflicts for Eastern European Jews: added to the danger of being forced to desecrate the Sabbath and disobey the dietary laws was the concern that these men, as the only earners in their families, would have to abandon their families to bitter poverty. They also justifiably feared harassment and had an aversion to serving a power that was exclusively devoted to repression. Attempts to escape military service are thus all too understandable. For this reason, births were either registered on a date that was more advantageous than the true one, or boys were registered as girls.

name first appears in 1908, as "Carl Baer, Head Clerk." With the help of his postal checking account number, which remained the same over the years, I was able to prove the identity of this Baer with others subsequently listed under different addresses and with different professions. In the Address Book for 1921 a postal checking account number is listed for the "writer" Karl Baer, then living in Neukölln. The same number can be found in a list of postal checking account customers in the year 1935 under "Karl M. Baer, Kleiststrasse 10" (actually 11).[5] This was the man my family knew.

Some time after 1945 and the end of the Second World War, this same individual wrote as "Karl Max Baer" to the Berliner Entschädigungsbehörde, the Berlin Restitution Office. In that communication, he states that he was born on May 20, 1885, not, as it turns out, in Eastern Europe, but in Arolsen, Waldeck, in today's western German state of Hesse. Shortly after finding this last document, I was able to obtain a birth certificate from Arolsen, which contained the name "Karl" without the second name Max. It took intensive efforts on my part to obtain a certified copy of the complete register of births for May 1885, however. Instead, I kept receiving copies of the birth certificate with the name "Karl Baer" and the May 20 date of birth. Only after years of trying was I able to see the register of births itself. No Karl Baer is listed. Rather, in an entry dated May 21, 1885, the birth of a female child, Martha Baer, daughter of the merchant Bernhard and his wife, Lina Bär née Loewenberg, is noted. On February 2, 1907, some twenty-two years later, the registrar Müller adds the following sentence to this entry: "The child Baer, entered in this register, is of the male sex, and has been given the first name Karl instead of the first name Martha. Registered on the basis of a court order issued by the Princely Magistrates' Court Arolsen, of January 8, 1907." It had, in turn, taken me some twenty years of research to discover that the

---

5. From Postscheckkunden im Bezirk des Postscheckamts Berlin; Verzeichnis 1935.

birth certificate for "Karl" had originally been made in the name of Martha—but at last I had definitive proof of the identity of the two.

It was very soon after the change was made in the registry of Arolsen that the newly minted Karl Baer published his memoirs under the (curiously English) pseudonym N. O. Body, which we can read as either "nobody" or "no body." In choosing the name, the Zionist Karl Baer must surely have had in mind a passage from Theodor Herzl's novel *Altneuland*, or *Old New Land*, first published in October 1902. In the first chapter of this utopian novel about a future Palestine, two men discuss a notice in a newspaper that reads: "Wanted: an educated, desperate young man willing to make a last experiment with his life. Apply N. O. Body, this office." One of the men says, "But I should like to know who this Mr. Body is, with his queer tastes." "It is no one." "No one?" "N. O. Body, nobody. Means no one in English."

"This book tells a true story," the author of the *Memoirs of a Man's Maiden Years* writes as his first sentence. Even as he protests to its truthfulness, he publishes the book under a pseudonym to avoid detection, and he disguises facts that might enable the reader to identify him. For this reason, he gives his birthplace as "Bergheim," a small summer royal seat in Saxony-Thuringia, although he asks the reader not to look for it on a map. In fact, Arolsen *was* a royal seat, although as we know, in the principality of Waldeck rather than Saxony-Thuringia, and it was probably local pride that led the author to allude to this in spite of all his efforts to make the place unfamiliar. There is, incidentally, a place called Bergheim in Waldeck, not far from Arolsen.

Our author writes that he was born on Whitsunday in 1884. By giving this date, he makes himself one year older, but neither in 1884, nor in his actual year of birth, 1885, does May 20 fall on the Christian holiday. May 20, 1885, did, however, correspond to the first day of Shavuot, the festival of the giving of the Torah on Mount Sinai, in the Jewish year 5645. This reveals a method that he uses throughout the book to make things unrecognizable: Body—in the book Nora, and later Norbert—has "translated" all things Jewish into rough Christian equivalences. Thus he says: "Our lineage is not German. Our fore-fathers came from France," claiming the outsider status of French rather than Jew. At one point, Body mentions a playmate, Lotti, with the surname Krumane—distinctly odd-sounding in German, but an anagram of the common Jewish surname "Neumark." (I have, how-ever, been unable to find proof that there was a family by that name in Arolsen at the time.)

In general, the author has done a skillful job of hiding clues; the text itself is coherent. There are, however, one or two minor inconsisten-cies. As an apprentice, for example, the memoirist helps uneducated fellow workers to write letters by transforming foreign words into German. It is implausible that people with insufficient schooling would know words of foreign origin rather than German unless "for-eign" is code here for Yiddish. And overall, one has the impression that the closer the story comes to the time of writing, the more the author has to be careful not to reveal himself. He is thus forced to use a more vivid imagination to change details toward the end of his nar-rative than when writing of his childhood and early youth. Even so, the author makes at least two exceptions. He calls the woman who frees him and becomes his first wife "Hanna Bernhardovna," and Hanna, as we know from the gravestone with which this essay began, was indeed the first name of Karl Baer's first wife. The second excep-tion is his naming of the lawyer Sammy Gronemann, who legally rep-resented Martha Baer during her sex change. Gronemann (1875–1952) was the son of the provincial rabbi of Hannover, and at the turn of the century established the provincial branch in Hannover of the Zionistische Vereinigung für Deutschland (Zionist Association for Germany). From 1906 on, he practiced law in Berlin. Whether Baer had become acquainted with Gronemann only then or at an earlier date must remain an open question. The fact that the acquaintance between the two men may have been older is hinted at by Body in his book when he writes that Gronemann "had once been recommended to me in another case." Gronemann, however, does not mention the name Baer in his own memoirs.[6]

*   *   *

In 1877, eight years before the birth of Martha/Karl Baer, the town of Arolsen had 2,460 inhabitants, most of whom were Protestant. Although there was a small Jewish community whose history begins immediately after the town's founding in 1719,[7] the number of Jews was very small, just 67 in the year 1887. The small-town atmosphere of Arolsen is well described by Helmut Nicolai: "During the time before 1900, if a new building was erected in Arolsen it was a special event that was talked about in the whole region."[8]

The half-timbered house at Kaulbachstrasse 8, where Martha/Karl was born and spent her/his childhood, still exists. Standing before it today, one can almost feel the agonizing narrowness of the town and can imagine the difficulties that would have been presented by the body of this infant, so different from that of all the other babies who had come into the world there. The author writes, "The midwife congratulated my mother on the birth of a splendid little girl and then called my father, to whom she said that the physical properties of the newborn were so strange that she was unable to decide to which sex the child belonged." In this context, it is almost understandable that the main concern of the father, a well-known member of the local Jewish

6. Samuel Gronemann, *Erinnerungen.* Taken from his unpublished work and edited by Joachim Schlör (Berlin: Philo, 2002), and Samuel Gronemann, *Erinnerungen an meine Jahre in Berlin,* ed. Joachim Schlör (Berlin: Philo, 2004).

7. Michael Winkelmann, *Auf einmal sind sie weggemacht: Lebensbilder Arolser Juden im 20. Jahrhundert* (Kassel: Gesamthochschul-Biblikothek, 1992), p. 16.

8. Helmut Nicolai, *Arolsen: Lebensbild einer deutschen Residenzstadt* (Glücksburg: Starke, 1954), p. 227.

community, was to make sure that "the doctor (by means of a hand-shake) and the midwife (by means of a large sum of money) would keep silent, so that this 'dreadfully disagreeable thing' should not become known in wider circles." Naturally, against this background, Baer had no desire to be identified by everyone as the author of the autobiography.

According to his book, after finishing school, Nora began an apprenticeship as a salesgirl in "Sellberg"—in all probability, Bielefeld. When, later in the book, Hamburg is mentioned, however, it is Hamburg that is actually meant. It was from there that Martha traveled to Eastern Europe to work on behalf of the B'nai B'rith lodge. N. O. Body translates this in his memoirs into work as a journalist for an American newspaper in Eastern Europe, and as journeys to Norway and Turkey. The author describes in detail his travels and lectures. He writes that he "found that large parts of the population were destitute. One could hardly imagine a more tragic situation. The female population in particular lives in abject poverty, and, as instructed, I focused on them."

Body describes his experiences but fails to mention the main reason for his mission to the East, which was to aid in the fight against white slavery. White slavery was widespread in large parts of Eastern and Southeastern Europe, so much so that it was a social problem of the first order. Jews were indisputably involved in the practice, and this fact was exploited for anti-Semitic purposes. Although white slavery was by no means an exclusively Jewish issue, it was nevertheless one that Central and Western European Jews had to face.

In Germany it was August Bebel, the chairman of the Social Democratic Party, who first publicly pointed to the problem in a speech before the German parliament on February 6, 1894. He spoke of "human trafficking" that "mainly proceeded from Hamburg." "What I am talking about," said Bebel, "is the continuing traffic of girls who are sent to countries outside of Germany for the purpose of satisfying lust . . . Some of these girls, those who come from Austria and Hungary, are Jewesses."[9] Bebel's speech attracted attention. Louis Maretzki, longtime president of the German B'nai B'rith lodges, mentioned Bebel and his speech in a lecture held on October 25, 1902: "That is why it is legitimate for us as Jews to devote ourselves to these matters," he said, "and that is why our Order, which has written the effort to elevate the social standing of the Jews on its banner, must direct its attention to these failings. In the year 1897, the Committee for the Fight against White Slavery was constituted. We owe thanks to our Brother [Gustav] Tuch, who has opened our eyes to the problem by pointing out this cancerous damage . . . and making efforts to alleviate it."[10]

In 1899, Gustav Tuch's son Ernst, then twenty-seven years old, had written a path-breaking article in the magazine *Israelitisches Familienblatt* which he called "White Slaves." He reported on an international conference on white slave traffic that had been held in London from June 21 to 23 of that year. The conference and the article caused a stir and were much talked about in Jewish circles. In the *Israelitisches Familienblatt* Ernst Tuch wrote: "What concerns us Jews in this affair . . . especially are two points: 1) that recently the market has been flooded with Jewish wares; and 2) the fact that a good percentage of the traffickers in girls are Jews . . . Let us work together to denounce those wretches and to render them harmless."[11] In his article, Ernst Tuch sought to "energetically encourage" the Jews in Galicia and Russia to support efforts to fight against the traffic in girls and thus contribute to saving them. They could not solve this problem alone.

9. Stenographische Berichte über die Verhandlungen des Reichstages. IX. Legislaturperiode. II Session 1893/94. Band 2, from the thirty-third session on January 23, 1894, to the sixty-third session on March 5, 1894, p. 1025.

10. Speech by Maretzki in the [Vereinigten Deutschen] Reichs-Loge, handwritten manuscript, State Military Archives of the Russian Federation, Moscow 769–3–13, pp. 2r.–2v.

11. *Israelitisches Familienblatt*, no. 29 (July 19, 1899), p. 3.

Could Martha Baer have read the article? A copy of it is to be found in the records of the Hamburg Committee for the Fight against White Slavery, which are now housed in the Russian military archives in Moscow.[12] These documents tell us that this committee and, above all, Gustav Tuch played an important role in our author's life.

At the committee meeting of December 22, 1902, Gustav Tuch reported, "At the recommendation of Dr. Arthur Kahn of Bonn, a young woman from Bielefeld, Fräulein Martha Baer, had requested that the committee provide her with funds so that she could study to become a doctor, as she intended to work in Galicia in this capacity, according to the principles of the committee, when she had finished her studies." Martha received the answer that the committee did not have the money to fund such studies, which would "take six to seven years," but the printed minutes of the meeting go on to say that under the condition that Martha Baer "agreed to be trained as a teacher of domestic science (which would take about one year) with the intention of later going to Galicia as a missionary, one could enter into further negotiations. Fräulein Baer had agreed to the latter." The meeting moved that "Martha Baer will be asked whether her guardian gives his consent to her training as a teacher of domestic science and later

12. There is extensive literature dealing with the RGVA archives in Moscow. I wish to list only the following here: Kai von Jena and Wilhelm Lenz, *Die deutschen Bestände im Sonderarchiv in Moskau*, Der Archivar 1992, pp. 457 ff.; George C. Browder, "Captured German and Other Nations' Documents in the Osoby [Special] Archive in Moscow," *Central European History* 24, no. 4 (1991): 424–45; idem, "Update on the Captured Documents in the Former Osoby [Special] Archive, Moscow," *Central European History* 26, no. 3 (1993): 335–42. Recently, a Russian inventory of the Osoby Archive, Moscow was made available: "Ukazatel' fondov inostrannogo proiskhozhdeniia i Glavnogo upravleniia po djelam voennoplennykh i internirovannykh NKVD-MVD SSSR Rossiiskogo gosudarstvennogo voennogo arkhiva," ed. W. P. Koslov and W. N. Kuselenkov (Moscow: Modelism, 2001).

working in Galicia. If so, she will be requested to present herself in Hamburg."[13]

At the meeting of January 21, 1903, Tuch further reports on Martha Baer from Bielefeld that he "recommended that she perfect her knowledge of domestic science. Her skills would then be sufficient for the work in Galicia."[14] Evidently pleased with the proposal, Martha came to Hamburg and presented herself in February 1903; the financial report of the Committee of February 22, 1903 mentions an expenditure of twenty marks, "travel costs for Fräulein Martha Baer, Bielefeld for the purpose of presenting herself."[15] Apparently, she made an excellent impression, for at the committee's cost Martha once again came to Hamburg, this time from Arolsen, in April at the latest, and even received "remuneration"[16] for that month. She had surely gone to Arolsen to obtain the necessary consent from her guardian, although I have been unable to establish who this was; Martha's father had died on May 27, 1901, though her mother continued to live in Arolsen until her death on August 4, 1921.

On April 7, 1903, Martha Baer registered with the police in Hamburg as a lodger. Her landlord was Eduard Levinson (1867–1925), residing at Wexstrasse 35, on the third floor. He worked as an editor at the *Israelitisches Familienblatt* and, at the same time, was secretary of the Hamburg Committee for the Fight against White Slavery.

When Body writes in his memoirs that the brother of his friend Lucie Lenstein "offered, as a supplement to our conversations, to guide me

13. Jüdisches (U.O.B.B.) Zweigkomitee des Deutschen National-Komitees zur Bekämpfung des Mädchenhandels, printed minutes of the meeting on December 22, 1902, RGVA Moscow 769–2–369a, pp. 149r.–149v.

14. Ibid., p. 150v.

15. Ibid., p. 163r.

16. Ibid. The entire sum "for the journey from Arolsen to Hamburg and remuneration for April" comes to 36.50 marks.

through the narrow streets and alleyways where the poorest inhabitants of Hamburg lived in sordid conditions," he is, in a way, uncharacteristically describing a recent reality without trying to make it unfamiliar. He goes on to write that "I saw the area at first by day, and then by night, too, as the life in those streets is most typical at night. We also passed through the streets where prostitutes are quartered. My companion graphically described the circumstances of these unfortunate human beings, who bear the yoke of personal exploitation and social ostracism." Perhaps the editor Eduard Levinson is the model for the Lenstein who accompanies Body.

Both Martha Baer and Eduard Levinson are cited in reports written by the Hamburg police, who kept their Zionist activities under surveillance. The police during this period meticulously analyzed the Jewish press. Thus we know that Martha was first mentioned in a newspaper in Hamburg on May 18, 1903, when the *Israelisches Familienblatt*[17] refers to a meeting of the Zionistische Ortsgruppe Hamburg-Altona (Zionist Local Branch Hamburg-Altona) that took place on May 11.[18] After reporting on internal organizational matters, the article continues, "It was decided not to pursue a special relief program in the aftermath of the terrible anti-Semitic events in Kishinev in our local branch, because it had come to the knowledge of the meeting that a comprehensive relief program of local Jewish organizations was being planned." A lecture followed, devoted to a retrospective look at the propaganda work of this Zionist group. In the ensuing discussion, it was debated whether it would be useful to set up a commission to further this work and whether Jewish women should be included in this body. "One of the women present, Fräulein Martha Baer, spoke warmly in favor of this."[19] Martha had quickly found her place in the

17. *Israelitisches Familienblatt*, Hamburger Lokalausgabe 6, no. 20 (May 18, 1903), p. 11.
18. Staatsarchiv Hamburg, Politische Polizei SA 559, Bd. 1.
19. Ibid.

Zionist effort and is among the signatories of an invitation to an evening of discussion on September 9, 1903.[20]

For his part, Gustav Tuch was able to report to his committee on May 3, 1903 that Martha Baer had prepared herself intensively for her future activities. She had, for a month, been taking "a course at the Jewish School for Domestic Science. In addition, she was taking private lessons with the headmistress of the Wolfson'sche School for Domestic Science" as well as a first-aid course. In addition to these activities, she was receiving "lessons in Jewish affairs from Rabbi H. Weiß."[21] According to Tuch, "in spite of her youth, her knowledge is very broad, and her facilities are strikingly keen, both characteristics that are very seldom so highly developed in a young girl of her age."[22] It is of interest to note that in his memoirs, Body puts exactly these words into the mouth of a professor who is tutoring Nora privately in Berlin.

After she had been living in Hamburg for a year, Martha is called a *Volkspflegerin*, or social worker, in the *Israelitisches Familienblatt*, and the readers are told that, together with two other women, she left for Galicia on May 1, 1904.[23] Other Jewish magazines, too, report on "the first deputation of social workers, consisting of three ladies, . . . which is to strive to raise the economic position of the Jewish population."[24]

A letter in the Moscow Military Archive is of some importance in our context. It was written by Gustav Tuch on behalf of the Hamburg

20. Ibid.

21. Jüdisches (U.O.B.B.) Zweigkomitee des Deutschen National-Komitees zur Bekämpfung des Mädchenhandels, printed minutes of the meeting on May 3, 1903, RGVA Moscow 769–2–369a, p. 161r.

22. Ibid.

23. Staatsarchiv Hamburg, Politische Polizei SA 669. The article is taken from *Israelitisches Familienblatt*, Hamburger Lokalausgabe 7, no. 18 (May 2, 1904), p. 4.

24. *Jüdische Volksstimme Brünn*, no. 10 (May 15, 1904), p. 5.

Committee on June 5, 1904, to the Grand Lodge and its president, Louis Maretzki, in Berlin. He reports that three missionaries have been sent to Galicia, including Martha Baer. She is to open a school for domestic science in Lemberg (L'viv) in the autumn. Tuch goes on to say that the two other "missionaries, after repeated and lengthy discussion with the bodies of the Lemberg [Jewish] community, the local associations and the influential persons there, and in full agreement with them, have put forward the proposal that Fräulein Mart[h]a Baer should return to Germany to give a full report. The matter was described as urgent." Tuch writes that Hamburg had agreed to the proposal.[25]

One can only guess what the reasons for this urgent return may have been. In any case, Martha came to Berlin after having stayed for only one month in Galicia, and spoke in public about her work. On June 12, 1904, representatives of various Jewish associations gathered in Berlin in a conference room of the Grand Lodge (U.O.B.B.) for Germany at Wilhelmstrasse 118 to join in and support the relief program for Galicia. Martha Baer, just returned from Lemberg, gave a report. She was accompanied by another missionary, Paulina Kohn.[26] We do not know how long Martha Baer stayed in Berlin. In all likelihood, she soon returned to Lemberg.

My mother's aunt Margarete may have attended the event on June 12, 1904 and become acquainted on that occasion with the missionary, whom she later met again in her circle of friends as both Martha *and* Karl. These friends, many of whom were early Zionists, were discreet as long as they lived, even though Martha/Karl himself seems at first to have been somewhat open about the whole affair of his changed identity. Proof of this is the fact that he dedicated a copy of his memoirs to the poet and prominent Zionist Theodor Zlocisti (1874–1943).

25. RGVA Moscow 769–2–369a, p. 193r.
26. Hectographed paper of the Hamburg Committee from June 1904. RGVA Moscow 769–2–369a, pp. 210–11.

This copy of N. O. Body's book, which was offered for sale by a secondhand shop in Jerusalem in 2003, is in my possession. The dedication, in which Baer remarks that the poem at the beginning of his memoirs has been taken from a volume of Zlocisti's poems,[27] is written in his own very characteristic handwriting. Thus it was no secret, at least to Zlocisti, that N. O. Body and Karl M. Baer were one and the same person.

Martha Baer reported in detail to the B'nai B'rith lodges about her work in Galicia and the problem of white slavery. It seems that these reports have not been preserved. However, we know of her activities from other sources. In a report written in 1906, we read that well "prepared, and blessed with good rhetorical skills, the missionary Mart[h]a Baer has been working in Lemberg for two years." She "took over the organization of the Association for the Protection of Women and Girls in Lemberg and was placed at the head of the Executive Board of this association . . . She traveled throughout Galicia and gave the committee valuable information about the conditions . . . in Tarnopol, Brody, Stanislau, Zlovczov, and the surrounding areas, and in Czernovitz and other parts of Bukovina as well."[28] In her lectures she spoke about, among other topics, the white slavery issue and what steps should be taken to deal with it. She also organized courses for illiterates and undertook many other activities.

We know that it was during her stay in Galicia that Martha Baer's fateful acquaintance with the married Beile Heilpern Waldberg began. When their own wedding took place on October 10, 1907, Baer had, of course, already undergone his change, and his memoirs had already appeared. Thus, friends were able to publish the following

27. Theodor Zlocisti, *Vom Heimweg: Verse eines Juden* (Brünn, 1903), p. 24.
28. U.O.B.B., Auszug aus den Verhandlungen der siebzehnten ordentlichen Sitzung der Großloge für Deutschland VIII, held in Berlin on March 25–26, 1906, pp. 81–83.

information: "Norbert O. Body, the author of the book *Memoirs of a Man's Maiden Years*, married Hanna Bernhardovna yesterday in Vienna, the same lady who plays such a prominent role in the last part of his book. Out of love for her, and with the help of excellent lawyers and medical doctors, he succeeded in persuading the Minister of the Interior to agree to change his personal registration to the male gender. Body now lives as a civil servant in Berlin."[29]

*　*　*

Rudolf Presber and Magnus Hischfeld, the authors of the foreword and epilogue, respectively, to *Memoirs of a Man's Maiden Years*, obviously knew the true story of N. O. Body. By writing their accompanying texts, they surely wanted to help ensure the memoirs' success and to smooth the path to a new life for Baer, in both psychological and material terms (we do not know whether Presber used his connections with publishers to help get the book printed). It may be assumed that it was the prominent sexologist Hirschfeld who introduced Body to Presber. Presber writes that he had been "asked to write a short preface to this strange book, which contains an account only of things that have been experienced and nothing that has been invented." A doctor "with whom I had literary matters to discuss," had come to visit him and brought along a young woman.

In his epilogue, Hirschfeld understandably does not go into any biological detail concerning Body. Rather, he uses the opportunity to present his fundamental position on a number of educational, legal, and general human matters. A few months before Body's book appeared, Hirschfeld had presented the case to an interested public for the first time. On November 29, 1906, he had described three instances of wrongly determined gender to the Gesellschaft für soziale Medizin, Hygiene und Medizinalstatistik, or Society for Social Medicine, Hygiene and Medical Statistics. The fact that Baer himself was present is clear from a remark made by Hirschfeld: "It would be

29. Monthly reports of the *Wissenschaftlich-humanitären Komitees* 6, no. 11 (1907): 219.

instructive if, after my lecture, you grasp the opportunity to speak to these three people yourselves, so that you may be able to form a personal opinion of them." The first individual whom Hirschfeld introduced was "a 21-and-a-half-year-old person who until now has lived as a girl, and from now on, with the permission of the authorities, intends to continue her life as a man, with a masculine name and wearing men's clothing. It seems to me," Hirschfeld continued, "to be the most practical way . . . of acquainting oneself with the case, if I present to you the expert report on this case, which I presented to the Minister of the Interior on October 20 of this year. I also wish to pass around a wax impression of her genitals, which was created by Herr Kasten, the moulage artist from the Lassar clinic."[30]

The expert report to which Hirschfeld refers is also mentioned by Body in his memoirs, albeit without the doctor's name. While it has not survived, large parts of it are most likely identical to some of Hirschfeld's other writings.[31] He also mentions two additional experts: Dr. Iwan Bloch and Dr. Georg Merzbach, the latter of whom admits in a review of the *Maiden Years* to having been consulted on the case.[32]

30. Magnus Hirschfeld, "Drei Fälle von irrtümlicher Geschlechtsbestimmung, Medizinische Reform," *Wochenschrift für soziale Medizin, Hygiene und Medizinalstatistik* 15, no. 51 (1906): 614. Together with the sculptor Heinrich Kasten (1842–1921), the Berlin dermatologist Oskar Lassar (1849–1907) built up a moulage collection in his clinic. After Lassar's death, most of the collection was sent as a gift to Hamburg. Today the Kasten moulages form the main body of the teaching collection at the Hamburg University Dermatological Clinic, Eppendorf. Approximately a thousand moulages that were not sent to Hamburg but remained in Berlin were destroyed by fire during the Second World War (http://www.dermatology.uni-kiel.de/moulagen.html). Cf. E. Sundhaußen, G. W. Korting, and C. E. Orfanos, *Moulagen: Eine medizinhistorische Ausstellung anlässlich des 17. Weltkongresses für Dermatologie 1987 in Berlin* (Berlin: Diesbach, 1987), p. 14. According to information I received from the Universitätsklinik Hamburg-Eppendorf (March 2005), Karl Baer's moulage could not be found. It was likely lost.

31. Magnus Hirschfeld, *Sexualpathologie: Ein Lehrbuch für Ärzte und Studierende* (Bonn: Marcus und Weber, 1918), 2:44–48.

32. *Monatszeitschrift für Harnkrankheiten* (Leipzig, 1908), pp. 101–4.

Hirschfeld calls his patient Anna Laabs, but there is no doubt as to her identity: "The . . . case is that of a man mistakenly taken for a woman," he later wrote, "who some years ago, under the pseudonym N. O. Body, published a description of his life under the title *Memoirs of a Man's Maiden Years*, which caused a sensation and was indeed quite educational. Before she sought refuge with me, she had been about to commit suicide together with her lady friend, a married woman who later became her wife."[33] The text of the expert report follows and concludes: "There cannot be the slightest doubt that the case of Anna Laabs is one of incorrect gender determination."[34]

From Hirschfeld's remarks we gain additional information about the biography of Martha/Karl Baer, for example: "Conflict was caused for her . . . after she had been working for some years . . . to the great satisfaction of her superior, when suddenly the rumor began circulating that 'Anna Laabs is a man in disguise.' Before this, she had already procured potassium cyanide in order to commit suicide together with her lady friend, because the difficulties that had to be overcome in order to be able to marry her seemed insurmountable."[35] Finally, he writes, "Immediately after his change, Laabs, his real name is, of course, no more Laabs than Nobody, married his lady friend, whose first marriage had ended in divorce while Laabs was proceeding with his sex change. In the course of the divorce, the court had considered the question whether sexual intercourse with a person who is thought to be a woman, but in reality is a man, should not be considered adultery. The husband had brought up this question when he was to be designated as the sole guilty party because of adultery committed by him; he gave as the reason for his infidelity his wife's relationship with her lady friend. Soon after Laabs had overcome these tremendous

33. Hirschfeld, *Sexualpathologie*, 2:44.
34. Ibid., p. 47.
35. Ibid.

difficulties and taken her as his wife, fate dealt him a new blow. She died of pneumonia after three months of marriage. Now a new trial began. The family of the woman, who had been quite wealthy, contested the validity of the marriage and the inheritance rights of the husband, alleging that he was not a man, or at least, had not been a proper husband. However, their point of view was not accepted, and they failed to achieve their goal. I have heard that Laabs, who has been working as a civil servant for years, has been happily married for the second time for quite some time now."[36]

*   *   *

The publication of N. O. Body's book met with a lively response. In reviews published in literary and medical magazines, the book was unanimously praised as educational. The most comprehensive review was written by P. Kempendorff in the conservative magazine *Der Türmer* (The Watchman), which was read by many middle-class families.[37] Kempendorff relates the contents of the book over several pages and shows how much he values N. O. Body's work: "The book goes straight to the heart. It does not wish to cause a sensation; it will grant those who are lascivious, and reach for it, little satisfaction. It describes a painful youth but does not deliberately display the pain, and it is this chaste reticence that timidly permits us a glimpse of the soul, which awakens our sympathy . . . What captivated me about this book was the strange fate of a human being, the suffering and struggling and final triumph of the poor creature, who was searching for his true self and found it. That is why I wish for the author that it may not be lascivious curiosity, nor cold scientific interest, but rather human sympathy that will win his book friends."[38]

36. Ibid., pp. 47–48.
37. *Der Türmer, Monatszeitschrift für Gemüt und Geist* 9 (Stuttgart, 1907): 495–99.
38. Ibid., pp. 498–99.

The majority of readers probably read the book otherwise, however, savoring the sensation that the text provoked in spite of Kempendorff's pronouncements. Evidence of this may be gleaned from the many new editions that appeared in quick succession after the initial publication and then never again. There were at least six printings of the book after 1907, followed by two silent film versions. The first of these was produced in 1912 under the title, *Aus eines Mannes Mädchenzeit* (Memoirs of a Man's Maiden Time). Then in 1919 came *Aus eines Mannes Mädchenjahren* (Memoirs of a Man's Maiden Years). Only the earlier film has been preserved, although at some point in time, the opening credits from the later film were attached to it.[39]

By the summer of 1907, the satirical weekly magazine *Lustige Blätter* had already published a satire of the book, further proof that Body's work was widely known.[40] Rudolf Presber happened to be closely associated with the editor in chief of the weekly, Alexander Moszkowski.[41]

* * *

Karl Baer continued to be interested in the white-slavery issue after the publication of his memoirs. In 1908, articles on this subject written by Baer appeared in journals edited by Presber and Hirschfeld. Whereas the article published in *Arena* edited by Presber is signed by

---

39. In this version, with the erroneous title *Aus eines Mannes Mädchenjahren*, the film is in the collection of the Stiftung Deutsche Kinemathek-Filmmuseum Berlin. Cf. Hermann Simon, "*Aus eines Mannes Mädchenzeit* (1912) und *Aus eines Mannes Mädchenjahren* (1919): Wer war der Mann und wer das Mädchen?" in *Pioniere in Celluloid: Juden in der frühen Filmwelt*, catalog from the exhibition of the same name in the Centrum Judaicum Berlin, ed. Irene Stratenwerth and Hermann Simon (Berlin: Henschel, 2004), pp. 207–13.

40. H. O. Chstetter (= Gustav Hochstetter), "Aus eines Mannes Dienstmädchenjahren," *Lustige Blätter* 22, no. 28 (1907).

41. Alexander Moszkowski, *Das Panorama meines Lebens* (Berlin: F. Fontane & Co., 1925), p. 97.

"M. Baer," the essay in the *Zeitschrift für Sexualwissenschaft* (Journal for Sexology) edited by Hirschfeld is signed "K. M. Baer-Berlin."[42] Also in 1908, more than a year after Baer had started living as a man, a book by M. Baer was published under the title *Der internationale Mädchen-handel* (The International Trafficking in Girls), no. 37 in the series *Großstadt-Dokumente* (Metropolitan Documents), edited by Hans Ost-wald. The publisher's advance notice announces, "Baer's book . . . goes far beyond the usual brochure literature; anyone who knows who M. Baer is knows, too, that the book does not contain general obser-vations, but rather practical experiences and experience, manifold results of devoted and untiring work in the service of the fight against white slavery over a number of years."[43]

At first, Baer found employment with the Victoria Life Insurance Company and later, from January 1, 1911 to November 15, 1920, with the Berlin Jewish Community, as the head of the office of the com-munity parliament among other positions. On December 1, 1920, he became director of the Berlin B'nai B'rith lodges. He continued to work there until they were forcibly closed by the Gestapo on April 19, 1937.[44] Karl and his second wife, Elza, began to make plans to emi-grate, at the latest, after he had been arrested by the Gestapo several times, tortured, and mistreated.[45]

42. M. Baer, "Mädchenhandel," ed. Rudolf Presber, *Arena* 3 (August 5, 1908): 449–555, and K. M. Baer-Berlin, "Über den Mädchenhandel," ed. Mag-nus Hirschfeld, *Zeitschrift für Sexualwissenschaft* 9 (1908): 513–28.

43. *Börsenblatt für den deutschen Buchhandel*, no. 134 (June 12, 1908), "Künftig erscheinende Bücher" (books to be published).

44. On the closing of the lodges, cf. Grete Baer, "Die Schließung der Berliner Logen U.O.B.B. im April 1937," eyewitness report by Grete Gitla Baer from February 2, 1959, Yad Vashem Archive, Jerusalem.

45. "The reason for the Gestapo activity was that they wanted to force us into admitting a connection between the B'nai B'rith lodges and the Commu-nists, which they were unable to do, because such connections never existed" (restitution documents, Karl Baer, Landesverwaltungsamt Berlin, Entschädi-gungsbehörde, AZ. 55 029; [Grete] Gitla Baer on February 18, 1958).

My maternal grandfather, the Berlin lawyer Hermann Jalowicz, wrote in his diary on July 24, 1938: "I called the Baers on the telephone. They are selling everything. I spoke with Miss Fisch [Baer's secretary]. Everyone is gloomy. They put love and thought into purchasing their things, and now they have to sell them off cheaply."[46]

On September 20, 1938, after taking leave of Karl Baer's sisters, who lived near Arolsen, Karl and Elza Baer emigrated to Palestine. There, Baer finally, after much difficulty, found work as a bookkeeper. Elza died on January 14, 1947 and Karl M. Baer married for the third time, in Israel on February 19, 1950. His new bride was his secretary, Grete Gitla Fisch, the Miss Fisch my grandfather mentioned in his diary. She had a close and intimate relationship with the Baers while Elza was still alive, and my mother told us that her family received postcards from the Baers that were signed, "Cordial greetings from Karl M. Baer, together with wife and Fräulein." It was general knowledge that this was a ménage à trois.

On June 26, 1956, Karl M. Baer died in Bat Yam, near Tel Aviv, and was buried under the name Karl Meir Baer in the Kiryat-Shaul Cemetery in Tel Aviv. The stone, on which only the date of his death and not of his birth appears, lies flat over his grave, like the one for his first wife, Hanna (Beile), in Berlin. More than forty-seven years and 1,800 miles lie between the dedication of the two stones, but they are bound together by a single story. I have tried to untangle this story and relate it so that the memory of the person who was both Karl and Martha may be kept alive. S/he wrote about her maiden years, which were so full of conflict, under the pseudonym N. O. Body, but s/he was somebody who has left a mark. Her/his struggle, achievements, humanity, and lively intellect deserve to be recorded and remembered:

"For every single man is a world which is born and which dies with him; beneath every grave-stone lies a world's history."

46. Diary of Hermann Jalowicz for the year 1938; in the possession of Hermann Simon, Berlin.